THE EVERYTHING®
COCONUT DIET
COOKBOOK

Dear Reader,

You may have tried several fad diets, and yet here you are, reading another diet book. Why? Low-fat diets requiring extensive calculations, specialized menus, and unfamiliar foods have been shown to be ineffective for most dieters. Restricting your body's access to important nutrients causes cravings for unhealthy foods that are almost impossible to ignore. Because of this, even if you lose a significant amount of weight on a restrictive diet, once you stop, you almost inevitably gain back all of the weight—plus more!

The coconut diet is not a traditional diet in the sense of restricting foods but a way of life based on traditional diets of indigenous peoples in tropical climates all over the world. Food should not be complicated. How can a person enjoy life if the focus is weighing food and meticulously counting each dietary unit? Eating should be a little like breathing—an enjoyable, relaxing, and essential part of living that does not require a calculator or a scale. Even if you make no other changes, using coconut oil is something you can do that will bring noticeable changes within a few short weeks. So here's to your better health!

Anji Sandage

Welcome to the EVERYTHING® Series!

These handy, accessible books give you all you need to tackle a difficult project, gain a new hobby, comprehend a fascinating topic, prepare for an exam, or even brush up on something you learned back in school but have since forgotten.

You can choose to read an Everything® book from cover to cover or just pick out the information you want from our four useful boxes: e-questions, e-facts, e-alerts, and e-ssentials.

We give you everything you need to know on the subject, but throw in a lot of fun stuff along the way, too.

We now have more than 400 Everything® books in print, spanning such wide-ranging categories as weddings, pregnancy, cooking, music instruction, foreign language, crafts, pets, New Age, and so much more. When you're done reading them all, you can finally say you know Everything®!

QUESTION
Answers to common questions

FACT
Important snippets of information

ALERT
Urgent warnings

ESSENTIAL
Quick handy tips

PUBLISHER Karen Cooper

DIRECTOR OF ACQUISITIONS AND INNOVATION Paula Munier

MANAGING EDITOR, EVERYTHING® SERIES Lisa Laing

COPY CHIEF Casey Ebert

ASSISTANT PRODUCTION EDITOR Melanie Cordova

ACQUISITIONS EDITOR Hillary Thompson

ASSOCIATE DEVELOPMENT EDITOR Hillary Thompson

EDITORIAL ASSISTANT Ross Weisman

EVERYTHING® SERIES COVER DESIGNER Erin Alexander

LAYOUT DESIGNERS Colleen Cunningham, Elisabeth Lariviere, Denise Wallace

Visit the entire Everything® series at *www.everything.com*

THE EVERYTHING COCONUT DIET COOKBOOK

The delicious and natural way to:

>> Lose weight fast
>> Boost energy
>> Improve digestion
>> Reduce inflammation
>> And get healthy for life

Anji Sandage with Lorena Novak Bull, RD

Adams media
Avon, Massachusetts

*To my daughter Alex; in hoping that you will
continue to choose the path of healthy living.*

An Everything® Series Book.
Everything® and everything.com® are registered trademarks of F+W Media, Inc.

Published by Adams Media, a division of F+W Media, Inc.
57 Littlefield Street, Avon, MA 02322 U.S.A.
www.adamsmedia.com

ISBN 10: 1-4405-2902-7
ISBN 13: 978-1-4405-2902-3
eISBN 10: 1-4405-3023-8
eISBN 13: 978-1-4405-3023-4

Printed in the United States of America.

10 9 8 7 6 5 4 3 2

Library of Congress Cataloging-in-Publication Data
is available from the publisher.

The information in this book should not be used for diagnosing or treating any health problem. Not all diet and exercise plans suit everyone. You should always consult a trained medical professional before starting a diet, taking any form of medication, or embarking on any fitness or weight-training program. The author and publisher disclaim any liability arising directly or indirectly from the use of this book.

Many of the designations used by manufacturers and sellers to distinguish their products are claimed as trademarks. Where those designations appear in this book and Adams Media was aware of a trademark claim, the designations have been printed with initial capital letters.

Nutritional statistics by Lorena Novak Bull, RD.

*This book is available at quantity discounts for bulk purchases.
For information, please call 1-800-289-0963.*

Contents

Acknowledgments

I would like to thank all of those who helped make this possible: I would like to thank Everything® series editor Hillary Thompson for giving me the opportunity to write this book and for her never-ending patience and attention to detail. I would also like to extend a special thank you to my friend Dr. Dave Altman, doctor of chiropractics and author of *Rethinking Health—How to Save Your Body, Mind, Spirit, and the World,* for his extensive help and expertise, especially with Chapter 3: Coconut Oil and Heart Health and Chapter 6: Immunity. Dr. Altman's e-book can be found as a free download from his website at *www.docaltman.com.*

I also want to thank my dear friend and sister, Denise Merrell, yoga instructor and mother of five, who has lived well with food allergies over the last several years, and who has children with food allergies and sensitivities, for sharing her own expertise and personal research in Chapter 4. And I especially want to thank my husband Fred, for helping clear my schedule and giving me the time I needed to write, and my children for not complaining about having been assigned the job of designated taste testers as we experimented with and tried out several new recipes together.

Introduction

THERE IS A REASON that people began calling the coconut palm the tree of life—the oil has wonderful antifungal properties that reduce candida and yeast overgrowth. Coconut oil can stop and even reverse mental deterioration caused by Alzheimer's and dementia brought on by aging. The meat is high in protein and provides a lasting energy source. Coconut water is full of electrolytes and is a hydrating source of refreshment, and the milk is full of fats, vitamins, and minerals that will add nutrient-dense elements to your recipes as well as body and flavor.

This book will help you by not providing a restrictive diet plan, which is almost impossible to follow in the long term, but by providing you with tools that you can use to create menus and plan meals that can be used for yourself and your whole family. You will learn a way of life rather than a diet with set menus and strange new foods. You can even learn how to adapt your own favorite recipes to make them healthier, tastier versions of the foods you love. If you have not previously been accustomed to cooking meals from scratch, this book will provide you with the skills you need to make preparation quicker and easier, with ways to make your own mixes and make-ahead ingredients that you can keep on hand for quick preparation later.

The recipes that you will find here will incorporate not only coconut oil, as many coconut diet books do, but you will find recipes that use all parts of the coconut and all of its various byproducts, including the meat, water, milk, flour, vinegar, and sugar. Each of these parts of the coconut are packed with nutrients that will enhance your health and provide much-needed nourishment that is too often lacking in the readily available processed foods that you have been using up to this point. Often, only a few small changes are needed to restore health and energy. Changing from vegetable oils and margarine to extra-virgin, unrefined coconut oil and other natural fats is one of the easiest things that you can do in your quest to improve your health. You can substitute coconut oil in a 1:1 ratio for any other fats or oils called for in most recipes. Even if you make no other changes in your diet, switching to coconut oil is something that will bring noticeable differences for most people within only a few short weeks. So, if you are willing to make the necessary changes, this could be the last diet book that you will ever need!

CHAPTER 1

Coconut Diet Basics

The coconut diet is based on traditional diets of indigenous peoples in tropical climates all over the world. Coconut dishes are traditional fare in Hawaii, Tonga, Samoa, Malaysia, Africa, South America, New Zealand, and many other places. Coconut oil, meat, water, milk, crème, sugar, flour, and vinegar are all byproducts that have been used throughout the ages in many parts of the world. Read on to discover how you can use this miracle food for maximum health benefits!

Why Choose the Coconut Diet?

Nature has provided foods in their original state with a variety of flavors, ranging from sweet to savory, salty, and sour. You should be able to enjoy eating all of these natural elements without feeling guilty. The coconut diet provides a way for this to become a reality, while at the same time helping you maintain a healthy weight. Choosing coconut products that are as fresh as possible and in their most natural unprocessed state gives you all of the benefits from this miraculous food!

Weston A. Price and Indigenous Diets

Dr. Weston A. Price was a dentist in the 1930s who became concerned with the growing number of cavities that seemed to be related to the increase in heart disease and other illnesses. He noticed that people who were healthier had fewer cavities and began to research what was in the modern diet that could be causing this problem. Dr. Price traveled around the world, studying indigenous cultures where people had been eating traditional diets for thousands of years. In his travels, he began to notice that the farther from civilization, the fewer cavities people had. In many of the cultures he studied, cavities and disease were very rare. This correlated with the amounts of processed foods that people were eating in those areas. Another striking commonality was the amount of unprocessed saturated fats that these people ate: between 40 and 80 percent of their total calories came from healthy fats like extra-virgin coconut oil, olive oil, animal fats, and full-fat unprocessed dairy products.

FACT

Dr. Weston A. Price's research is published in his book *Nutrition and Physical Degeneration*. In 1999, a foundation was formed based on his extensive nutritional research, the Weston A. Price Foundation. More information on the Weston A. Price Foundation can be found at *www .westonaprice.org*.

The Big Fat Lie

In the early 1900s, new technologies provided increasingly widespread use of commercially canned foods and other highly processed foods such as white flour, white sugar, refined iodized salt, and hydrogenated shortening. Due to the consumption of these new foods, modern-day illnesses began to appear at a rate previously unheard of. Heart disease, cancer, digestive issues, cavities, crowded teeth, and other serious health concerns inspired Weston A. Price to research these problems.

As he traveled around the world and studied traditional diets, one common factor he found was that healthy populations consumed between 40 and 80 percent of their calories from fats. In a standard American diet, the USDA food pyramid previously recommended only 35 percent of calories come from fats, and with the recent re-evaluation, has further restricted this recommendation to as little as 20 percent. With these dietary recommendations, it has become increasingly more difficult to get enough fats in your diet, especially because foods that are naturally high in fats have been stigmatized as "fattening, must-avoid" foods. Healthy foods such as coconut and palm oil, nuts, seeds, avocados, butter, and natural animal fats have been replaced with processed, "food-like substances" filled with trans fats. These highly processed vegetable oils, hydrogenated and partially hydrogenated oils, and artificial fat replacers are made with the goal of increasing shelf life and appealing to health-conscious consumers who, ironically, choose low-fat foods because they have been led to believe that they are healthier choices. This is tragic, because these wholesome fatty acids are essential for weight loss and the absorption of fat-soluble vitamins like A, D, and E as well as water-soluble vitamins like C. All of these vitamins are essential for proper immune function and sustaining life.

ESSENTIAL

These fatty acids also help you absorb minerals like calcium, magnesium, and boron, all of which are essential for strong bones and the prevention of osteoporosis. These minerals, along with iodine, are essential for proper thyroid and adrenal function and enhance mental clarity and prevent depression and mental deterioration in old age.

In spite of all the research pointing to these benefits, the average American continues to gain weight, and diet-related health concerns such as heart disease, diabetes, obesity, and digestive problems continue to increase at a steady rate. Even so, popular dietary recommendations continue to demonize and restrict healthy fats.

Low-fat foods have become so prevalent that even a person who is not trying to diet may unwittingly end up eating a low-fat diet. How? Because meats are now automatically trimmed of fat—ground beef is almost always 85 percent lean, chicken is boneless and skinless for convenience—and manufacturers have reduced the amount of fat in their products to appeal to consumers who choose low-fat or fat-free products in their efforts to make healthier choices. In fact, because of how deeply the low-fat craze has permeated our culture, you really have to work consciously at getting more than 20 percent of your calories from fat, and you have to work even harder to get a balance of healthy fats in your diet.

Coconut as a Traditional Food

Coconut has been used for centuries in many cultures around the world as a diet staple. Coconut is so engrained in these cultures that it is hard to identify any one particular way it is used, but here are some highlights from tropical cultures around the world.

Polynesia

In the Polynesian Islands, coconut cultivation by the inhabitants dates back over 3,000 years. Specific dishes vary from island to island, but the diet mainly consists of seafood, coconut, and tropical fruits. Some examples of coconut dishes in the Polynesian culture are marinated raw fish with coconut cream, and fish wrapped in coconut leaves and then roasted in a pit in the ground. Coconut oil is used for frying foods, and fibers from the husks are used to make ropes and fishing nets. In New Zealand, where there is room for larger-scale farming and raising of cattle and pork, meats are braised in coconut milk with ginger, very similar to Malaysian dishes.

Hawaii

Coconut is believed to have been brought to Hawaii by Polynesian travelers, and quickly became part of the Hawaiian culture. Not only did they use the coconut water and meat, Hawaiians extracted coconut oil, used the shells to make drums, and used the fibers for cleaning teeth, weaving nets, and as covers for their boats.

Malaysia

Malaysian cuisine is very similar to Indian food, and uses rice steamed in coconut milk. This coconut milk rice is often served with anchovies, sliced cucumber, peanuts, and hard-boiled eggs seasoned with a spicy chili paste. Seafood and chicken curries, served with flatbread, as well as vegetable or mutton stews cooked with coconut milk are common fare.

FACT

One of the first recorded instances of coconut was in 1500 B.C. in Ayurvedic texts, which highlighted the healing properties of coconut oil.

Africa

In many African cultures, coconut milk and curry are also common. In some parts of Africa, popular dishes contain a combination of coconut milk, peanuts, and bananas. Coconut milk is widely used in soups and to cook vegetables, egg dishes, fish, meat, and poultry. Coconut milk is also used to cook rice and cornmeal porridge.

South America

In several South American cultures, coconut milk is often used to cook rice and beans. Fish stews made with coconut milk and seasoned with chili peppers, cumin, and cilantro are popular as well as different varieties of white fish cooked in coconut milk and served with a coconut sauce. One example of a popular South American dish is chicken slow-cooked in coconut with lime, jalapeños, and cilantro and served with rice.

The Philippines

Like many other cultures, in the Philippines, the people make use of every part of the coconut. Brooms made from the ribs of coconut leaves, bound together in a bundle or a fan, are widely used. Whole coconut leaves are used as roofing materials, coconut shells are used as fuel for fires, and in Filipino cuisine, coconut is everywhere. Young coconut meat or *buko* is a popular snack, while coconut oil is widely used for frying, and coconut milk is used for cooking seafood, rice, vegetables, and stews.

Anatomy of a Coconut

Coconut is a very sustainable crop because even though it takes a long time for the fruit to form, coconut trees are continually blossoming and forming new fruit, so there is a year-round harvest available. Coconuts are made up of several components, all of which have long-standing historical uses in many cultures:

- **The outer husk:** Used as fuel for fire, and to make ropes, fishing nets, brushes, and mats
- **The shell:** Coconut shells have been used for making bowls and utensils and as containers to drink from.
- **Coconut meat:** High in protein; can be used to make coconut milk and cream
- **Coconut water:** Coconut water is the liquid inside the coconut. It is sterile and can actually be used as a replacement for blood transfusion.

Coconut byproducts include:

- **Coconut milk:** Coconut milk is made by puréeing coconut meat with water and then straining out the pulp.
- **Coconut cream:** Coconut cream rises to the top of coconut milk, and has a higher concentration of fat. It can be skimmed off of the top in the same way that cream is skimmed from animal milk.
- **Coconut oil:** There are several ways that coconut oil is extracted: by pressing, through centrifugal force, through heat extraction, and through chemical extraction. It goes without saying that you will want to avoid coconut oil that has been extracted by using chemicals, and methods that use extreme heat should also be avoided. When buying coconut oil, check the label to see what it says about the extraction process. If it doesn't say anything, then you probably want to avoid it

because companies that use safe and healthy means to extract the oil will place it on their label.

Two ways to extract coconut oil through pressing are expeller pressing and cold pressing. Expeller pressing forces coconut meat through a corkscrew press. This process creates a lot of friction, and even though this is not a heat extraction method, the press does generate heat, anywhere between 140°F to 210°F. This isn't enough to damage coconut oil, since coconut oil is very stable and can be used for frying without being damaged, but it can't be considered raw. Another downside to expeller-pressing coconut oil is that it can only extract about 75 percent of the oil, so there is a lot of waste.

Cold pressing uses a press to extract oil from coconut meat. The pressure does create some heat, but still well below temperatures that would cook it—only about 113°F.

Coconut can also be extracted using centrifugal force by placing fresh coconut in a centrifuge with hot water, then spinning the coconut at high speeds to separate the oil, the solids, and the coconut milk. This method uses varying temperatures, so you need to read the label if you want raw coconut oil.

- **Coconut flour:** Coconut flour is made from the meat of the coconut that has had most of the oil extracted, then is ground into a fine powder. Coconut flour is gluten free and high in protein, but can yield very crumbly results, so many recipes using coconut flour also call for a lot of eggs.
- **Coconut sugar:** Coconut sugar is made from the dehydrated "sap" of the coconut flower.
- **Coconut vinegar:** Coconut vinegar can be made either from the sap from the coconut flower or from fermented coconut water. The best coconut vinegars have live cultures.
- **Coconut aminos:** Coconut aminos are made by fermenting the sap of the coconut flower in much the same way that soybeans are fermented to make soy sauce. Coconut aminos are a salty, soy-free alternative and can be used in recipes that call for soy sauce.
- **Coconut fiber:** Coconut fiber from the husks of the coconut can be used to start fires and to make nets, ropes, brushes, and other useful things.

- **Coconut shells:** Coconut shells have been traditionally used to make dishes, drinking vessels, and eating utensils.

Choosing a Fresh Coconut

It is not always possible to get fresh coconut in good condition. If you have a coconut tree in your back yard, great! But most people have to rely on what they can get at the supermarket, and unless you know what to look for, you will most likely get a few "bad eggs." Of course, fresh coconuts are best if you can get them, but there are also many good organically produced coconut products that are still very healthy and can be used to make delicious coconut dishes.

To select a coconut, choose a coconut that feels heavy, that does not have cracks, and that, when you shake it, you are able to hear liquid splashing inside. It should sound and feel full. Do not choose coconuts that are moldy or that feel damp or moist around the eyes.

If you live in an area where coconuts grow, you can check for them in your local farmers markets. The only places that coconut grows in the United States without irrigation are Hawaii and Florida. The following is a start for places you can look:

- **Florida**
  U.S. Department of Agriculture Farmers Market Search:
  http://apps.ams.usda.gov/FarmersMarkets
  www.frugalicity.com/Florida-farmers-market.html
- **Hawaii**
  http://hawaii.gov/hdoa
  Kauai Farmers Markets
  www.realkauai.com/FarmersMarkets

Choosing Coconut Products

When purchasing coconut products, look for the ones that have been the least processed. For example, look for extra-virgin organic coconut oil and shredded coconut that does not contain added sweeteners. Always check the labels and avoid coconut with additives. Dry coconut can be reconstituted by soaking it for 30 minutes in coconut milk to make it more like fresh grated coconut.

ALERT

Just because a product has coconut in it doesn't automatically add it to a list of good-for-you products. Many coconut products are highly processed and refined. In our world, where there are many confusing messages about how to eat and be healthy, it is important to be discerning. Learn to read labels and make the best choices possible!

The following resources are good places to buy coconut products online:

- **Wilderness Family Naturals**
  www.wildernessfamilynaturals.com
  Wilderness Family Naturals sells extra-virgin coconut oil, coconut milk and cream, coconut water, coconut spreads, flaked coconut, coconut flour, coconut sugar, and coconut vinegars.
- **Tropical Traditions**
  www.tropicaltraditions.com
  Tropical Traditions sells high-quality extra-virgin USDA organic coconut oil as well as raw, organic coconut-water vinegar, coconut peanut butter, coconut flakes, coconut cream, and coconut flour.
- **TIANA Fair Trade Organics**
  www.tiana-coconut.com
  TIANA sells a complete range of USDA organic coconut products, including coconut flour, extra-virgin coconut oil, desiccated coconut, coconut milk, coconut cream, and cream of coconut.
- **Simply Coconut**
  www.simplycoconut.com
  Simply Coconut sells raw USDA organic, extra-virgin coconut oil. They also carry coconut flour, shredded coconut, palm oil, and books by Dr. Bruce Fife on the health and nutritional properties of coconut.
- **Coconut Secret**
  www.coconutsecret.com

Coconut Secret sells high-quality USDA organic coconut aminos, coconut vinegar, coconut sugar, and coconut flour.

- **Artisana**
  www.artisanafoods.com
  Artisana sells raw organic coconut oil and coconut butter.
- **Green Pasture**
  www.greenpasture.org
  Green pasture carries USDA organic extra-virgin coconut oil and coconut ghee.

Tools and Techniques

So you've gone to the grocery store, and you have in your possession a brown, hairy ball with a shell that you can't seem to penetrate with your kitchen knife. Before you go and accidentally cut yourself or ruin your newly acquired coconut, it's a good idea to get a few tools. You will need a glass, a hammer, a nail or awl, and a hand towel.

The easiest way to open a coconut is with a hammer and a thick nail or awl. Get a hand towel and fold it in fourths. Set the coconut on the towel with the two or three dark indentations, or eyes, facing up. Hold the coconut steady with one hand, and press your nail into one of the eyes so that it stands up on its own. Then use the hammer to pound the nail into the coconut's eye. Repeat this step with the other eyes.

Fresh coconuts that have not been opened can be stored at room temperature for about four months. If you purchased your coconut at your local supermarket, they are probably not all that fresh, and you will want to keep them in the refrigerator where they will stay good for up to two months. The best way to store coconut is to open them, grate the coconut, and then keep it in the freezer, where it will last up to six months.

Then, place the coconut holes down on the glass to let it drain. If it drains too slowly, you can punch a hole into the bottom end of the coconut to let more air in, but this will be a little harder to do than it was to punch a hole where the coconut eyes are because of the shell, so make sure you hold the coconut steady and watch your fingers!

Once the coconut water has drained out, wrap the coconut in the hand towel and give the coconut a couple of good whacks with the hammer to break it open; then you can remove the coconut meat. Use a paring knife to peel off the brown outer skin of the coconut meat. Then cut it into chunks or grate it with a cheese grater. Use it immediately or store it in the refrigerator in an air-tight container for later use.

Storing Coconuts

Grated fresh coconut will last six months if it is stored in a sealed container or a re-sealable plastic bag in the refrigerator or freezer. Dry packaged coconut from the store can be kept at room temperature for six months, but once the package is opened, it needs to be refrigerated and will last about a week. Canned coconut milk can be stored on a shelf in your cupboard or pantry for eighteen months. Coconut oil can be kept at room temperature for up to two years, and does not need to be refrigerated.

CHAPTER 2

Weight Loss

If you have tried every diet there is and you still have not lost weight, maybe it's time to dump diets and try a lifestyle change instead. Coconut is a very effective tool for weight loss, and coconut oil has many benefits that will help you lose weight. There are many reasons that people can't lose weight, but as a society, we tend to dwell on the ones that have been beaten into our heads—the ones that will give us the most guilt. For example, you didn't stick to your diet. Forget that the diet was impossible—who can live on 1,200 calories a day? Yet, you probably beat yourself up because somehow you were supposed to be able to do it—like the amazingly skinny woman down the block. She lives on 1,000 calories a day and does aerobics constantly. So why can't you do it, too? Well, for one, she is nuts and you are normal. So what *can* you do?

Wait—Won't Saturated Fats in Coconut Oil Make Me Fat?

Eating saturated fat by the tablespoon? It's crazy talk! Well, it may seem that way considering all of the conditioning that we go through in our current society. Low-fat products have become so prevalent now that even a person who is not trying to diet may unwittingly end up eating a low-fat diet.

The next time you go grocery shopping, pay attention to fat percentages of common foods. Our bodies need saturated fat to build cell walls, for proper brain function, and to help us drop unwanted pounds. Eating saturated fat is also necessary for proper metabolic function. Eating saturated fat, especially coconut oil, actually slows down the process that our bodies use to store fat. Saturated fat slows down the absorption of sugars in the bloodstream, which are often stored as fat in the adipose tissue if there is more than the body can use at one time.

What Causes Weight Gain?

So, if it's not the fat, what is it? There are several things that can cause weight gain. Weight gain can be caused by a sluggish thyroid, slow metabolism, not eating often enough and at the right time of the day, prediabetes, adrenal fatigue, depression, and "healthy" low-fat dieting. Yes, that is right. Most likely, the weight problem is not caused by overeating. Most people do not overeat as much as they just eat the wrong kinds of food, and this isn't all their fault—look at the dietary guidelines that we are given. Low fat, and lots of grains; half of those grains are allowed to be unhealthy processed foods—and this is what is taught since elementary school.

The medical community touts a low-fat, high-carb diet, and instead of fixing the problem by adjusting the dietary guidelines to reflect the findings of years of research on the subject, they continue to go back to the same unhealthy standard, represented by a new graphic. This balance of foods sets up a climate of unquenchable cravings in the body. And it ricochets out of control with a cycle of "being good," where you suppress your cravings, trying not to make eye contact with the cake that a coworker brought to work, to binging—giving in to the cravings that you have been fighting all day long. Busy schedules prevent regular meals, and you end up feeling guilty and beating yourself up, which leads to depression binging. Then you get back to "being good," and the cycle repeats.

So if it isn't as simple as overeating, what is it? The following things are the most common problems faced by dieters, and how the coconut-diet lifestyle can help you beat them:

Eating the Wrong Foods

Probably the most common mistake in dieting is eating a "healthy" low-fat diet. It is possible to lose weight this way; however, very few people are able to do so and keep off the weight because the lack of dietary fat causes carbohydrate cravings that undermine the diet process. These cravings also cause other health issues like dry itchy skin, hair loss, and dry brittle nails. Sixty percent of Americans are overweight. Most of these people have probably been on a diet at least once in their lives, yet low-fat, restrictive-calorie diets only have a 5 percent success rate. So yes, it is possible, but not for the majority of dieters. The reason that low-fat restrictive diets often do not work is because restricting fat throws you onto the merry-go-round, so to speak. Low-fat diets deplete your body of important nutrients, and as a result, your body rebels. Then begin the cravings, the binging, the guilt, the depression, and the periods of staunch discipline where half of the time you are preoccupied with thinking about food. That is not living!

ALERT

When you do buy coconut oil, ghee, butter, and rendered animal fats, make sure they do not contain hydrogenated or partially hydrogenated fats.

The first thing that will bring true success is throwing the calorie-counting notebook out the window. Then go through the pantry and take out all of the food. Anything boxed will probably need to go. Refined sugar and flour—gone. Replace any iodized processed salt with unrefined sea salt that is not plain white—it should have some color to it—either gray, pink, or speckled. Then replace those things with real food. A variety of whole grains—not just whole-wheat flour, but other grains and seeds, as well. And coconut products that are whole and as fresh and unprocessed as possible, without added sugar. And last but not least, take back the fat. You have been told long enough that you can't have it. Dump the fake fats: margarine, Crisco, and processed vegetable oils. Get the ones that actually taste good: coconut oil, ghee, butter, and rendered animal fats. Remember, this is a lifestyle, not a diet, so taking some time to replace the processed foods in your pantry will make the transition a lot easier.

Not Eating Regular Meals and Not Eating the Right Foods at the Right Time

The second thing that needs to be done to establish an eating lifestyle is to establish a regular meal routine. It is easy to get caught up in a hectic schedule and forget about eating, but not eating enough can actually slow your metabolism and cause weight gain.

The second part to this is timing. Eating too many high-carb foods later in the evening is more likely to cause weight gain. Making sure that your meals have at least 40 percent of your calories from healthy fats like coconut oil will give your meals more staying power, will boost your metabolism, and will leave you more satisfied and less likely to have cravings for unhealthy foods. It is not necessary to count calories; just estimate and stick to reasonable serving sizes. If you avoid any simple carbohydrates, like fruits, after 4 P.M., you will begin to lose weight, even if you eat after that time. If you get hungry, have some tender young coconut meat as a snack.

Sluggish Thyroid and Depression

Ten percent of Americans most likely have an undiagnosed thyroid disorder. If you are experiencing unexplained weight gain, fatigue, hair loss, insomnia, depression, and anxiety, you could have an undiagnosed thyroid disorder. Thyroid disorders can lead to serious problems, but very often the doctor will tell you to get more sleep or put you on antidepressants because your basic thyroid hormone levels came back within the normal range. Often thyroid disorders get overlooked because without the proper testing, they can be hard to detect. If you suspect that you have a thyroid disorder and you don't get a diagnosis because your doctor didn't order a full thyroid panel, you should get a second opinion. Adding coconut oil to your daily routine can also have a positive effect on the thyroid, and can even reduce or eliminate hypothyroidism.

Coconut oil has the effect of balancing thyroid production, whether you have hypothyroidism or hyperthyroidism. One theory is that perhaps coconut oil, with its unique medium-chain fatty acids, improves the body's ability to use fats and sugars by raising the metabolism and stabilizing blood sugar levels in the body.

In her book *Eat Fat, Lose Fat*, Dr. Mary Enig writes, "While no studies have investigated how coconut oil affects the thyroid gland specifically, the fact that it raises body temperature and causes weight loss indicates that it supports thyroid function." Eating whole, unprocessed foods and adding real fats to the diet will have a profound effect on a thyroid disorder, but coconut oil is especially beneficial to the thyroid. Depression is often a symptom of hypothyroid disorder, and will usually go away after the thyroid picks up its pace.

Adrenal Fatigue

Adrenal fatigue occurs when the adrenal system has been under excessive stress and begins to shut down, lowering production of vital hormones that prevent you from feeling your best. Adrenal fatigue can cause weight gain and a suppressed immune system. Coconut oil and a diet of whole natural foods that are free of chemicals will go a long way to help those with symptoms of adrenal fatigue.

Prediabetes

Prediabetes is completely reversible with a whole-food diet that contains plenty of coconut oils and other coconut products. If you are prediabetic, stick to real foods and use at least 2–3 tablespoons of coconut oil per day.

How Is Coconut Oil Different from Other Saturated Fats?

Coconut oil is different from other fats in that it is made up of medium-chain fatty acids (MCFA) and lauric acid, which are harder for the body to convert into larger fat molecules for long-term storage. This is because coconut oil bypasses the regular route—instead of waiting to be processed and turned into glucose by the digestive system, it can go straight into the cells and be used as fuel immediately. Not only does this raise your metabolism to help you burn more fat, it is not stored on the body as fat, either.

FACT

After reviewing some of the data regarding coconut-eating groups, Hans Kaunitz and Conrado S. Dayrit, MD, found that the available population studies showed that dietary coconut oil does not lead to high serum cholesterol or high coronary heart disease mortality or morbidity. Islanders from the Philippines and Polynesia who had high levels of coconut oil consumption in their diets showed no evidence of a harmful effect from the coconut oil they consumed on a daily basis. (*A New Look at Coconut Oil*, Mary G. Enig, PhD)

Studies conducted on the effects of eating coconut oil that claimed it causes high cholesterol and heart disease were flawed because they used partially hydrogenated coconut oil. This oil has been damaged, and does not have the same healthful effects on the body as unrefined coconut oil. Unfortunately, these studies led to the medical community's current stand against it as a saturated fat, since they believed that there was no difference between hydrogenated oils and unrefined oils.

How Does Coconut Oil Help with Weight Loss?

Coconut oil and coconut work to help you lose weight by stabilizing your blood sugar levels and raising your metabolism. Replacing any margarine and other trans fats with coconut oil is one of the most important steps in following a coconut diet because the trans fats actually cause inflammation and prevent you from losing weight. Getting rid of processed foods is a very important step because most processed foods contain hydrogenated or partially hydrogenated oils, even if the package says no trans fats.

Omega-6s and Omega-3s

Also, avoid any processed foods that contain vegetable oils like corn or soybean oil. These oils are high in omega-6, which your body does use, but most people get so many omega-6 fatty acids in their diets that the ratio of omega-3 is off balance. Most people get three times the amount of omega-6 in their diets than they should; even if they never use vegetable oils, they get them from seeds and grains. Extra omega-6 in your system causes inflammation and makes it difficult to lose the extra weight.

Replacing these unhealthy oils with coconut oil helps to bring your essential fatty acids (EFAs) into balance. Coconut oil doesn't contain any omega-3 oils, but it also does not contain omega-6 EFAs, either. Coconut oil has a unique structure that allows your body to have the saturated fats that it needs without raising the number of omega-6 EFAs. Coconut oil also helps the body use omega-3 EFAs more effectively, enhancing them and their effects in your system. Coconut oil goes directly to the cells and is used immediately as energy, causing an increase in metabolism and helping your body use stored fat.

Reducing Your Cravings

Eating coconut oil also helps you lose weight by making you feel full longer and helping reduce food cravings for things that will cause weight gain, like simple sugars and refined flour. Using high-protein coconut flour will allow you to have a few baked items without all of the extra carbohydrates. Coconut flour is high in protein and has a good, mild flavor compared to some other types of low-carb flours.

CHAPTER 3

Coconut Oil and Heart Health

For those who are unfamiliar with the benefits of coconut oil, the first thing they think of is their fear of saturated fat. The next most common response is the fear that lots of saturated fat will cause a heart attack. These two concepts have been so thoroughly drilled into the deepest recesses of our brains that the following information may make your head spin.

Coconut Oil Can Make Your Heart Sing

Conventional wisdom is that saturated fat and cholesterol plug the arteries, eventually breaking off and causing a heart attack. Case closed. Well, not so fast. Think about this:

- In 1900, heart attacks were nearly nonexistent, and people ate a lot of saturated fat.
- In the 1930s, heart attacks were causing about 3,000 deaths per year.
- By the 1960s, heart attacks were causing 500,000 deaths per year, and the population was eating significantly *less* saturated fat.

When you look at those simple numbers, there should be some alarm bells going off in your head. There has to be more going on than conventional wisdom, and there is. So why the big jump in deaths? Something else was happening, and it had nothing to do with saturated fat consumption. People were actually eating less saturated fat. One of the major factors was a higher consumption of sugar. Before the 1900s, sugar was a luxury item made from sugar cane. New technology allowed for beet and corn sugars to be processed cheaply, and soon the sugar bowl was a regular addition to the dinner table. After World War II, processed grains, convenience foods, and new oils made from vegetable seeds were flooding the store shelves.

FACT

In the Philippines, where heart disease accounts for about 8 percent of hospital patients, coconut oil is an integral part of the people's diet. Research performed comparing regions of the Philippines found that in the region where coconut oil is consumed at the highest rate, nearly 2 tablespoons per day, there was also the lowest mortality rate from heart disease. Heart disease in the Philippines is one of the lowest in the world, and most cases are linked to rheumatic fever, not fat consumption.

Overcoming Saturated Fat Fears

Why is there such a fear over saturated fat? In the 1940s, when heart attacks started becoming more common, there needed to be a reason for it. The medical establishment believed that as arteries closed down with plaque, the blood flow to the heart muscle was compromised. If the blood flow was cut off long enough, a heart attack would follow.

ALERT

Dr. Uffe Ravnskov, an independent researcher in Denmark, questioned the validity of Ancel Keys's lipid hypothesis and began to examine data from past research to discredit the idea that any one dietary fat could be any worse than all of the others. He did not believe that saturated fats could be the sole cause of heart disease, and wrote the book *The Cholesterol Myths* in 1991, disputing Keys's findings and showing that mortality rates due to heart disease were not directly related to fat consumption. When he came out with his book, he was ridiculed by the media.

The medical community didn't have a known cause for this until the 1950s, when Dr. Ancel Keys came up with the theory that cholesterol was the problem. By analyzing the fat consumption of twenty-two nations and comparing the death rates from heart disease, he came to the conclusion that saturated fat was the culprit. But his study was flawed. One of the most serious flaws, and perhaps the most telling of the entire theory, is that he used only the six countries that supported his case that fat consumption led to heart disease. If all twenty-two nations had been used, the link between fat and heart disease would have all but disappeared.

FACT

One news channel actually set Ravnskov's book on fire on live television. His book was not published until 2000, when his work was noticed by the Weston A. Price Foundation.

In the beginning, there was much doubt from fellow researchers and doctors, but once the American Heart Association began publishing their findings, this view became the norm. For the next fifty years, it has remained essentially unchanged. This misguided advice of a "heart-healthy diet that is low in fat" has put the United States on an appalling path to rampant obesity, type 2 diabetes, cancer, and heart disease. The biggest factor leading to these wild increases in disease and obesity was not saturated fat consumption but the increased consumption of processed grains, sugar, and vegetable oils.

Drawing Your Own Conclusions

You are ultimately responsible for what you eat and how you live. If you still think saturated fat or cholesterol is the enemy, then consider reading *Ignore the Awkward: How the Cholesterol Myths Are Kept Alive*, Dr. Ravnskov's current book on the subject. (*The Cholesterol Myths* is currently out of print.)

QUESTION

Where else can I read about the lipid hypothesis?
Dr. Uffe Ravnskov is only one of several independent researchers who questioned the lipid hypothesis, a theory that tries to explain weight gain and heart disease as a symptom of saturated fat consumption. Some of the other scientists who have performed research to refute Keys' Lipid Hypothesis are Anthony Colpo, author of *The Great Cholesterol Con: Why Everything You've Been Told About Cholesterol, Diet, and Heart Disease Is Wrong!*; Daniel Steinberg, MD, PhD, author of *Cholesterol Wars: The Skeptics vs. the Preponderence of the Evidence*; and Malcom Kendrick, MD, author of *The Great Cholesterol Con: The Truth About What Really Causes Heart Disease and How to Avoid It.*

The War on Saturated Fats

The war on fat and cholesterol is still in full swing, so naturally coconut oil is under fire. In 1988, Congress actually met to discuss the safety of tropical oils. Surgeon General C. Everett Koop called the attacks on coconut oil "foolishness." Unfortunately, the coconut-producing countries have a very weak lobbying effort compared to the vegetable oil giants in the United States. Coconut oil, once widely used, was eventually replaced by hydrogenated vegetable oils.

FACT

Coconut oil does not need to be refrigerated. It is so stable that it can be stored at room temperature for up to five years without refrigeration. Unsaturated oils used in cooking foods are unstable, and even cooking at relatively low temperatures cause these unsaturated oils to become more unstable, making them become rancid in just a few hours. Eating foods that contain rancid oils increases free radical activity that speeds aging, causes inflammation, and causes disease.

The irony is that coconut oil is very stable, able to sit on a shelf for years, whereas processed vegetable oils go rancid and oxidize fairly quickly sitting on a store shelf. It makes you wonder why companies who make snack foods use hydrogenated vegetable oil to increase the shelf life of their products when coconut oil is far more stable and has a much longer shelf life compared to hydrogenated vegetable oils. What it really came down to was cost. Hydrogenated vegetables are far cheaper to produce.

The Impact of Vegetable Oils

Now when you visit a U.S. grocery store, vegetable oils are what await the unknowing consumer. This has been a major contributing factor to the rise of heart disease since the 1950s. The free radicals flow through the blood vessels, slamming into the walls, and creating a lot of damage. Your body deals with this damage by patching the holes with cholesterol in an attempt to fix the problem. Since the average American diet is filled with these trans fats, the body is just doing its best to heal you with what it has available: poor-quality fats! The often-demonized cholesterol is nothing more than an innocent bystander who witnessed the car wreck of vegetable oils and rushed in to help the injured, only to be accused of murder.

Why Coconut Oil Can't Clog Your Arteries

The *Philippine Journal of Cardiology* asked this very question: Why can't coconut oil clog your arteries? The Philippines? Yes, you should also look outside the United States to get more information. The United States only consumes about 0–2% of daily calories from coconut oil. If you consider countries that actually consume coconut in large amounts, you can find some answers. In the Philippines, nearly everyone consumes coconut oil on a daily basis.

Dr. Dayrit, of the *Philippine Journal of Cardiology*, reviewed 119 articles and original studies and came to one conclusion. All the people who consume coconut oil on a daily basis have low cholesterol levels and low rates of heart disease when compared to those who do not.

ALERT

Research studies show that environmental toxins are one of the common risk factors in developing heart disease. One reason that coconut oil can help prevent heart disease is that it has the ability to neutralize some environmental toxins. A study published in 2005 in the *Journal of Human and Experimental Toxicology* showed that coconut oil was effective for neutralizing aluminum phosphide, a toxin used as rat poison. One case study examined a situation where a man ate a lethal dose of aluminum phosphide in an attempt to commit suicide. Doctors had little hope that he would live, and he was given coconut oil along with the standard treatment for poisoning. Much to the surprise of the medical staff, the man survived. Regular consumption of coconut oil has a detoxifying effect, and can help cleanse your body of toxins that may adversely affect heart health.

The Philippines are broken up into many islands and regions. The Bicol region is famous for its coconut-flavored dishes and has the highest coconut oil consumption in the Philippines. People in this region consume an average of 26 grams daily. That is about 2 tablespoons per person per day. If you compare that to the 16 grams the Manila region consumes and then compare the overall death rates caused by heart disease between the two regions, the Bicol region had the lowest death rate.

As an interesting side note, they brought in a second group of researchers to look at cholesterol. All the regions had cholesterol levels below 200, but the Bicol region, where deaths due to heart disease were lowest, actually had the highest cholesterol levels. This further illustrates that the cholesterol levels had absolutely nothing to do with heart disease. So, what is really important here? The only effect that the rate of coconut oil consumption had on these people was the lower the rate, the higher the incidence of heart disease.

When researchers added up all the Filipino mortality from heart disease and compared that to fat consumption, just as Ancel Keys did in his analysis when he was trying to pin fat consumption to heart disease back in the 1950s, the results were in favor of coconut oil. If plaque in the arteries is caused by eating fat, as Keys postulated, then the Filipinos should have been off the charts. Yet, their death rate from heart disease is the lowest in the world, even lower than Japan's.

Medium-Chain Fatty Acids

Almost all of the coconut oil you consume doesn't even enter into the cholesterol cycle. How is that possible with all that saturated fat? Coconut oil is made up of about two-thirds medium-chain fatty acids (MCFA). These fatty acids behave differently than the long-chain fatty acids (LCFA) found in animal fats. Unlike LCFAs, the MCFAs of coconut oil are quickly absorbed by the intestines, very similar to the speed with which sugars are absorbed. Once in the body, the MCFAs are shuttled right to the liver and directly burned for energy. The LCFAs need pancreatic enzymes in order to be absorbed by the intestines, and then they have to go through a much longer process before they reach your liver to eventually be used for energy, cholesterol, sex hormones, adrenal hormones, cell membrane parts, vitamin D production, and myriad other useful things. You can think of MCFAs as gasoline used to quickly ignite a fire, while LCFAs are more like the bigger logs that keep the fire burning.

Your heart will thank you for using some coconut oil. If you are concerned about heart disease (and in America it is a very legitimate concern), then don't fret about using coconut oil. The much larger concerns are the amounts of sugar, grains, and vegetable oils that you consume.

Lauric Acid

Brent Muhlestein, a cardiologist at the LDS Hospital in Salt Lake City, Utah, was the first to discover that arterial plaque often contains bacterial pathogens. Further research using animal studies showed that infecting rabbits with chlamydia bacteria caused arterial walls to thicken considerably. After these rabbits were administered antibiotics, the arterial walls reverted back to their normal size. The reason that this is important is that along with the MCFAs, coconut oil also contains a significant amount of lauric acid. When lauric acid enters the body, it is converted to a monoglyceride compound called monolauren, which has antiviral properties. Monolauren in the body specifically targets bacterial infections and viruses like herpes, measles, influenza, hepatitis C, and HIV.

If you are concerned about heart health, coconut oil is an absolute must! Adopting a healthy whole-food lifestyle with a diet rich in healthy fats like coconut oil will go a long way toward helping you prevent heart disease. For optimum benefit, it is necessary to use cold-pressed virgin coconut oil and to avoid highly processed coconut oil that has been partially hydrogenated. It is also very important to eliminate all hydrogenated and partially hydrogenated trans fats and other unhealthy oils from your diet, because unlike coconut oil, they truly have been linked to obesity and heart disease.

CHAPTER 4

The Allergy Solution

Your immune system's job is to defend against potentially harmful intruders like viruses, bacteria, and toxins. Once in a while, your body identifies a particular food as a threat that would normally be harmless. Then your immune system responds in defense against the intruder, causing a wide array of symptoms. Coconut water, coconut milk, and coconut oil are known to help reduce these attacks because of their medium-chain fatty acid (MCFA) structure, which can help calm the intestinal tract and ease the symptoms of food allergies. Taking coconut oil daily and including plenty of coconut products in your diet along with other healthy whole foods is a good way to help combat food allergies, along with the other suggestions covered in this chapter.

Allergy Dangers

With more severe allergies, it is necessary to use food substitutions to replace common foods in order to reduce symptoms that make it hard to function from day to day. It is a good idea to get to know the foods that may be causing the problems. Many children are sensitive and may have an allergic reaction to certain foods, but they are likely to outgrow their allergies with the proper precautions. People who have never had allergies may also develop them over time.

ALERT

Sixty percent of Americans are suffering from some form of food allergies. If you are suffering from gastrointestinal distress, bloating, joint and muscle pain, hives or skin rashes, eczema, runny nose, headaches, anxiety, insomnia, dry itchy skin, or asthma, you may have a food allergy.

Did you know physicians have suggested that up to 60 percent of the American population is suffering from some form of masked food allergy? Often, people do not even realize that the symptoms they are dealing with on a daily basis are allergy related. However, with a little sleuthing, you can track down the food that is disrupting your system. Cutting the offending food out of your diet will usually eliminate those irritating symptoms.

Common Food Allergens

So, you want to know which foods are the chief offenders? There are eight different foods on the top of the list that account for 90 percent of all food allergies: milk, eggs, peanuts, tree nuts, fish, shellfish, wheat, and soy.

Food allergies most often develop with repetitive use, and can develop in people as they get older. Many of the foods that Americans eat on a regular basis have some form of dairy, wheat, corn, or soy in them. Convenience foods and prepackaged goods are especially loaded with these ingredients because they are inexpensive and easily available. Watch out, though, because some of these top offenders often assume an alias. For example, dextrose is a sweetener that is most often derived from corn in the United

States, but one wouldn't know that without a little detective work. Learning to read labels and keeping updated on all known food aliases is a crucial skill when it comes to avoiding those pesky allergies.

Some food aliases for the eight most common allergens are as follows: milk—lactose, eggs—albumin or ovalbumin, wheat—bulger or durum flour, soy—natto, miso, or edamame.

Signs and Symptoms

Some foods come crashing into your system, and there is no doubt in your mind that you should stay away from them! These food felons cause immediate symptoms. The reactions will typically show up within a few hours after eating the offending food, or even in just moments, causing obvious symptoms such as an itchy mouth, stomach cramps, diarrhea, a rash, hives, runny nose, headache—the list goes on. In very rare instances, the airway can swell shut, creating a life-threatening condition called anaphylactic shock.

However, most often, the foods that cause distress are stealthy. These types of allergies are much more difficult to track down because a delayed reaction occurs. Some of the symptoms can include: abdominal pain, indigestion, ear infections, sinus congestion, asthma, joint inflammation, headaches, dermatitis, fluid retention, dark circles under the eyes, memory loss, mood swings, anxiety, and depression. These symptoms can become chronic and in time cause other more serious conditions, even leading to disease.

Diagnosing Allergies

Apprehending a masked allergy takes a little detective work. If you chronically experience any of the symptoms previously described, it may be worth investigating a little further. The typical methods to track food down allergies include consulting an allergist or using an elimination or rotation diet.

A Rotation Diet

To help alleviate reactions due to food allergies, your doctor may put you on a rotation diet. Even if it is not prescribed, a rotation diet is a good idea because part of what caused allergies to develop is eating the same foods all the time. Even with a coconut diet, it is a good idea to rotate a variety of foods to avoid developing allergies to coconut. A rotation diet helps you avoid eating foods from the same biologically related group, or food family, too often. For example, to rotate foods from the nightshade family, you would only eat foods from this group once every four days—potatoes on one day, tomatoes four days later, peppers four days later, and so forth.

ESSENTIAL

Using a rotation or elimination diet may seem like a lot of trouble, but it is not nearly as much trouble as dealing with mysterious symptoms like hives or migraines that can crop up with no warning, making a normal life almost impossible.

Consulting an Allergist

An allergist will ask you questions about your symptoms and may administer a skin test or blood test. The skin test is performed by administering a small dose of the top allergens just under the skin of the arms or back. A blood test can also be used at times to determine the source of an allergy. They will help you determine whether or not you have an allergy by observing and measuring the reaction that occurs and by recording your responses. These methods can be helpful to get an idea of where to begin your search. However, sometimes the results are not completely accurate, and some foods and/or substances simply will not be tested; it would be impossible to test for every allergen.

Discovering Allergies by Elimination

The best way to uncloak an allergy is through the process of elimination. You begin with a food journal, then start an elimination diet by only eating foods that are known to be hypoallergenic or nonallergens. These foods get the good citizen award for being the least likely to cause an allergic reaction.

FACT

Skin tests can give a sense, based on the severity of the reaction to an allergen, of how severe your reaction might be to a particular substance. Blood tests or RAST (radioallergosorbent testing) measures the amount of antibodies in your body to a particular food. This may give an inaccurate test result if you are tested for a food that you have not eaten in a long time. Also, RAST testing is more expensive and can take up to two weeks to get your test results back, whereas the skin tests are immediate.

Foods That Cause Few Allergies

There are some foods that cause relatively few allergies. Here is a list of some foods with a low incidence of allergic reactions:

- **Coconut products**
- **Grains:** rice, amaranth, quinoa, millet
- **Sweeteners:** maple syrup, brown rice syrup, coconut sugar
- **Fruits:** apples and pears
- **Vegetables:** spinach, kale, lettuce, broccoli, cauliflower, Brussels sprouts, cucumbers, carrots, peppers, celery
- **Beans and legumes:** black beans, kidney beans, garbanzo beans, navy beans, lima beans, pinto beans, lentils, peas
- **Meats:** lamb, Alaskan salmon, unprocessed turkey with no injected fluids

Food Journaling

Begin a food journal. Log any symptoms you notice, even if you might not recognize it as a symptom per se (for example, being overly emotional). Log anything out of the ordinary that you observe for a week, things such as unusual emotions, headaches, gas, bloating, congestion, and cramping.

Begin your elimination diet by eating only foods from the foods with few allergens listed above for a minimum of two weeks. Keep recording your observations in your journal. When the two weeks are up, begin adding one new food back into your diet every four days. Continue recording symptoms you notice or that you realize are gone. Place the food offenders in lockdown and eliminate them from your diet! You will find that you will feel much better.

Regulation by Rotation

Even if you do everything you can to avoid food allergens, you just might find that you have to keep putting more and more foods into lockdown. The reason for this lies in the fact that the more commonly used a food is, the more likely an allergy will develop. The regulation of diet through rotation isn't just for those who suffer from food allergies; everyone can benefit from a rotating diet. This way of eating serves more than one purpose. First of all, you will get the nutritional benefits from a variety of wholesome foods, and you will avoid developing food allergies altogether. If you already have allergies, you may find that you can regain and increase your tolerance for the foods that you have had to ban from your diet. Sounds like a win-win situation!

Mandate Variety

Instead of habitually eating all the same grains, fruits, vegetables, dairy products, and meats, mix it up a bit by eating a variety of different foods. The idea behind a rotation diet is to eat foods from different food families over a four-day period. Here is table of different food families and their members:

▼ **PLANT FAMILIES**

Family	Food Types
Apple	apple, pear
Citrus	lemon, lime, orange, grapefruit, tangerine
Plum	plum, peach, apricot, cherry, nectarine, almond

Family	Food Types
Rose	strawberry, raspberry, blackberry, bramble berries
Heath	blueberry, cranberry
Mint	peppermint, spearmint, oregano, basil, sage, rosemary, thyme, balm, marjoram, savory
Ginger	ginger, turmeric, cardamom
Laurel	cinnamon, bay leaf, avocado
Myrtle	allspice, clove
Lily	onion, garlic, asparagus, chives, leek
Parsley	carrot, parsnip, celery (seeds), anise, cumin, coriander, caraway seed, fennel
Pea (Legume)	pea, black-eyed peas, dry beans, green bean, soy bean, lentils, licorice, peanut
Buckwheat	buckwheat, rhubarb
Gourd	pumpkin, squash, watermelon, cucumber, cantaloupe
Nightshade	tomato, potato, red pepper, bell pepper, eggplant, cayenne, paprika
Mustard	mustard, turnip, radish, horseradish, cabbage, broccoli, cauliflower, Brussels sprouts, Chinese cabbage, collards, kale, watercress, rutabaga, kohlrabi
Goosefoot	spinach, Swiss chard, beet
Sunflower (ragweed)	lettuce, endive, artichoke, dandelion, sunflower seed, tarragon
Grass (Grains)	wheat, corn, rice, oats, barley, wild rice, bamboo shoots, millet, sorghum, brown cane sugar, molasses
Mallow	okra, cottonseed
Fungi	mushroom, yeast
Cashew	cashew nut, pistachio, mango
Walnut	walnut, pecan, butternut
Cola Nut	chocolate (cocoa), cola
Palm	coconut, date

▼ ANIMAL FOODS

Family	Food Types
Mammals	beef, lamb, pork, rabbit, venison, cow's milk, goat's milk
Birds	chicken, eggs, turkey, duck, goose, pheasant, quail
Fish	tuna, salmon, catfish
Mollusks	oyster, clam, scallop
Crayfish	shrimp, lobster, crab

These foods are not related to each other, or any other foods:

▼ PLANT FOODS WITHOUT RELATIVES

banana, pineapple, papaya, fig, gooseberry and currant, grape, brazil nut, chestnut, hazelnut, macadamia nut, coffee, honey, vanilla, wintergreen, black and white pepper, nutmeg and mace, olive, sweet potato, tapioca, tea, flaxseed, maple sugar, persimmon, poppy seed

ALERT

Food allergies can be caused by any type of food, even some you might not expect, like beef, pork, chicken, cranberries, or sesame seeds . . . anything can cause an allergic reaction. This is why it is important to do some sleuthing—one person's list of allergens can be completely different from another person's, even if they are in the same family.

Defensive Meal Planning

The key to success is in planning. Now that you are armed with a list of foods from different families, begin planning your meals a week at a time, organizing each day with various items from different food families. Make sure that if you use a food from one family, you don't repeat using that food family for another four days. If this task seems daunting, there are cookbooks on the market that are there to help you learn how to stick to a rotation diet with lots of fabulous recipes and a schedule.

Coconut is not a common allergen, so including coconut products like coconut oil and milk daily should not be a problem for most people. However, if you are very sensitive to foods and have many food allergies, eating coconut every day could cause you to develop a food allergy to coconut. If you are on a rotation diet for severe allergies, only use coconut products every four days, just as you would for other food families.

If you are not dealing with severe food allergies, you may wish to try a simpler approach by adding a wide variety of foods to your diet, including using coconut oil and coconut milk for cooking. Coconut aminos are a great substitute for soy sauce, and coconut vinegar can be used in place of distilled white vinegar, since most white vinegar is made from corn byproducts. Coconut milk can be substituted for dairy if you are allergic to animal milks, and coconut sugar can be used instead of other corn-based sweeteners. Begin by using foods that are currently in season; mix it up with different colors, textures, and tastes. Give old standbys a break and add new tastes and nutrition to your fare. Here are some ideas that can get you started:

- **Butters/Spreads:** Besides peanut butter, enjoy coconut butter, almond butter, coco-hazelnut spread, pea butter, sun-seed butter
- **Flour:** coconut, almond, amaranth, barley, bean flours, buckwheat, corn, kamut, millet, nut flours such as almond and hazelnut, potato, quinoa, rice flour, sorghum, spelt, tapioca, teff, whole-wheat pastry flour
- **Milk:** coconut, goat, hemp, nut milks such as almond and Brazil, oat, rice
- **Oils:** coconut oil, avocado, flaxseed, grape seed, olive, palm, peanut, rice bran, safflower, sesame, sunflower, walnut. (Note: oils should be used sparingly and should be organic and cold pressed. Be sure to avoid heating liquid oils other than olive oil, which can be used for sautéing. Most liquid oils should be avoided or used in cold recipes like dressings only. Corn oil, canola oil, and soy oil should especially be avoided because they are almost always highly processed, and corn and soy are two of the most common allergens.)
- **Sweeteners:** Brown rice syrup, date sugar, fruit concentrates, local raw honey, maple syrup, palm/coconut sugar, stevia, sucanant

QUESTION

What are the best web resources for food allergies?
As food allergies become more and more commonplace, some great resources have emerged. Here are a few good websites for dealing with food allergies: Allergized—Take Control of your Food Allergies: *www.allergized.com*; Kids With Food Allergies Foundation: *www .kidswithfoodallergies.org*; The Food Allergy and Anaphylaxis Network: *www.foodallergy.org*; Help & Hope—How to survive with multiple food allergies and eventually thrive again: *www.food-allergy.org*; Food Allergy Initiative: *www.faiusa.org*.

Deliciously Peaceful Living

Food is such a big part of our lives—after all, we eat throughout the day! Not only is it a necessity, it becomes an aspect of our social life, as well. Learning that you or your loved one has a food allergy can be a huge emotional challenge. It is hard to change the way you eat and live. The good news is that there is a lot of support for those learning to live in harmony with their food allergies. The web is alive with really great resources—cookbooks that can be purchased or checked out at your local library and blogs and various articles written about the very same struggles that you are facing. Educating yourself will help you find that there really is a whole new world of food just waiting for your taste buds to relish. So enjoy!

CHAPTER 5

Diabetes

Coconut's unique properties go a long way in helping maintain health in people with diabetes. Besides lowering blood sugars, in some cases, coconut has completely reversed symptoms of type 2 diabetes with only 2–3 tablespoons of coconut oil per day. Coconut can help relieve, and in some instances completely stop, neuropathy; it can improve circulation and restore feeling to limbs where numbness has set in. It can improve blood sugar regulation and eliminate hunger and cravings.

What Is Diabetes?

Diabetes is a metabolic disease where the body either does not produce enough insulin or does not respond to the insulin that is being produced. There are three basic types of diabetes:

- **Type 1:** Type 1 diabetes is an autoimmune disease caused when the body will no longer make insulin. Treatment for type 1 diabetes includes daily insulin replacement, usually through injections, and strict monitoring of blood sugar levels. A person with type 1 diabetes cannot live unless he has insulin shots every day.
- **Type 2:** Type 2 diabetes is caused by insulin resistance, or a condition where the pancreas makes insulin, but the body cannot use it. Type 2 diabetes is managed through a strict diet and constant monitoring of blood sugar levels as well as medications to help the body recognize insulin in the bloodstream. If needed, insulin injections or an insulin pump—if insulin levels drop too low—may also be required. The majority of people who have diabetes have type 2.
- **Gestational diabetes:** Gestational diabetes is when a pregnant woman who did not have diabetes before pregnancy has high blood glucose levels during pregnancy. Gestational diabetes is treated through diet, exercise, and closely monitoring blood sugar levels. This type of diabetes usually goes away after the baby is born, but women who develop gestational diabetes are at risk for developing type 2 diabetes, which can be avoided through a healthy diet and exercise.

Diabetes and Traditional Diets

In his article "Diabetes and Virgin Coconut Oil," Bruce Fife, ND, describes the rate of diabetes in the Pacific islands and the connection to traditional diets—ones that included fresh fruits, vegetables, and an abundance of coconut products. Fife explains that those who abandoned this traditional diet succumbed to numerous health problems, including type 2 diabetes. Refined flour, sugar, and processed vegetable oils replaced the traditional bananas, coconuts, and yams, and the result was the emergence of type 2 diabetes. Fife concludes this article with a startling example from the World Health Organization: Up to one-half of the urbanized population in the island of Nauru aged thirty to sixty-four are now type 2 diabetic.

Diabetics are at higher risk for heart disease because not only do they need to avoid simple carbohydrates, trans fats and many vegetable oils intensify this problem. Since most liquid vegetable oils cannot be heated without causing the chemical structure of the oil to oxidize or go rancid, there are not very many oils that diabetics can safely use. Coconut oil is one oil that diabetics can eat because it can be utilized by the body without the need to produce insulin.

Using a traditional diet is very beneficial for diabetics—if the food or oil was not used 100 years ago, then it probably has no place in your pantry, and most vegetable oils were not around in those days. If they were, consider a traditional diet to see how those oils were used.

FACT

Diabetes is caused by the body's inability to regulate blood sugar by either an inability to create or use insulin. Coconut oil is a great blood sugar stabilizer—it helps those with diabetes by decreasing the stress on the pancreas and helps provide energy to the body because it is absorbed easily without insulin or enzymes.

Fats that were used for cooking 100 years ago, depending on what part of the world you lived in, were rendered animal fats, coconut oil, olive oil, and butter. These fats were used regularly in much higher amounts than what is used today, during a time in history where diabetes and heart disease were nonexistent to rare.

Liquid oils, like nut oils or seed oils, were only available in small amounts and were not generally used for cooking the way they are today. Some oils did not even exist in the human diet until very recently, like soy, corn, and canola oil, as well as hydrogenated and partially hydrogenated versions of these and other oils. Interestingly enough, these new oils seem to correlate with the rise in type 2 diabetes and heart disease. Is there a connection? You decide.

Type 2 Diabetes Can Be Induced by Diets High in Vegetable Oils

In his book *The Coconut Oil Miracle*, Bruce Fife mentions some research done in the 1920s, where a class of medical students consumed a diet high in modern-day vegetable oils. This diet triggered reversible diabetes in forty-eight hours! Since this classroom experiment, researchers have been able to duplicate this several times on test animals simply by feeding them diets high in polyunsaturated vegetable oils, then reversing the disease by taking those oils out of their diets.

According to Dr. Fife, coconut oil is the only oil that diabetics can eat without having to worry about their health. Fife explains:

> *Not only does it not contribute to diabetes, but it helps regulate blood sugar, thus lessening the effects of the disease. The Nauru people consumed large amounts of coconut oil for generations without ever encountering diabetes, but when they abandoned it for other foods and oils the results were disastrous.*

Why Polyunsaturated Oils Can Contribute to Type 2 Diabetes

When a person is diagnosed with type 2 diabetes, one of the first recommendations from her doctor is to eat a diet low in fat, where the fats are limited to polyunsaturated vegetable oils. The problem with this is that these fats have now been proven to be a major part of the cause of type 2 diabetes. They also cause inflammation, free-radical damage, and they suppress the immune system, allowing the body to be vulnerable to all kinds of disease.

About Polyunsaturated Oils

Over the last fifty years, in trying to prove they were the solution for heart disease, clogged arteries, and high cholesterol, polyunsaturated fats have been studied extensively. Early studies came out showing that polyunsaturates reduced cholesterol levels and therefore the risk of heart disease, but the larger experiment continues to show that these oils actually cause the very things that they are touted for preventing.

The first study aimed at proving that removing saturated fat from the diet would improve the overall health of society was conducted by Dr. Ancel Keys, who "presented a perfect curvilinear correlation between the mortality from coronary heart disease and the consumption of fat in six countries" (*The Cholesterol Myths* by Uffe Ravnskov, MD, PhD), but his research was based on a group of countries that he cherry picked to fit the hypothesis he formulated at the beginning of his project. Even in subsequent studies by other researchers, his perfect curve has not been duplicated. By the time that others discovered his data was skewed, it was too late. The study had already been publicized and the media ran with it, using his "research" to build polyunsaturated fatty acids up into the golden calf of the health industry, seducing the American public with claims that these oils are "heart healthy" and can prevent everything from heart attacks to obesity.

The truth is, that because of the structure of polyunsaturated oils, they are far less stable than saturated fats, especially coconut oil, which is very stable. These oils also have the ability to trigger type 2 diabetes because as the cell membranes swap out lipids from healthy fats and bring more polyunsaturates into the structure of the cell, that cell becomes less and less able to bind to insulin in the bloodstream, making your cells unable to absorb glucose. Since glucose is the primary energy source for cells in the body, as a result, polyunsaturates are effectively starving you to death, cell by cell.

ALERT

Polyunsaturated oils have been shown in studies to trigger type 2 diabetes. The good news is that it is reversible in most cases. Removing these oils from your diet and replacing them with coconut oil can help you recover.

Fortunately, this effect is reversible, and once you eliminate polyunsaturates from your diet and replace them with healthy fats like coconut oil, cell membranes begin to replace the lipids with healthy fats, making your cells able to bind to insulin and utilize glucose from the bloodstream. While polyunsaturates can slow down metabolism, coconut oil increases it, helping you not only burn off the coconut oil that you just ate but also taking some of your stored fat with it.

How Coconut Oil Reverses the Effects of Type 2 Diabetes

Imagine being able to reverse the effects of type 2 diabetes—to be able to reduce or even eliminate the amount of prescription medications that you are currently taking. Coconut oil has a number of beneficial properties that make it ideal for reversing the effects of type 2 diabetes. Its unique structure allows it to act like glucose to feed your body on the cellular level, boosting your metabolism and powering up your immune system with its healing properties. Its ability to improve blood circulation and reduce numbness and neuropathy make it ideal for those who suffer from the effects of type 2 diabetes.

Coconut Oil Nourishes the Body

Normally, when you eat something, your digestive system breaks it down and converts it to glucose. The glucose enters your bloodstream, which triggers your pancreas to make insulin. Insulin attaches to a cell and then helps bring the glucose into the cell, where it is used as energy. With diabetics, either the insulin does not get created or it cannot attach to the cells, which causes the cells to be unable to absorb and utilize glucose.

Coconut oil does not need insulin to be absorbed by the cells and to be used as energy. Your body can use the medium-chain fatty acids in coconut oil in much the same way as it can use glucose, but it doesn't require insulin to do it. This allows the pancreas to rest, allowing it to heal, and in some cases, recover the ability to make insulin.

Metabolism

Because of the problems with absorbing glucose, a common problem with type 2 diabetes is lower energy levels and weight gain. Without the glucose to power your cells, your metabolism slows down and your energy level drops. Coconut oil can counter this effect because of the way that it is used by the body. As coconut oil is absorbed by the cells, it boosts the metabolism, allowing your body to burn more fat faster. It also slows your digestion and allows you to feel fuller longer. Because coconut oil can be used so quickly by the cells, it creates a burst of energy, which then increases metabolism and your energy levels, and aids in weight loss. Several research studies have been done on metabolism and coconut oil, and studies showed decreased body fat in rats and in humans.

Blood Sugar Regulation

If your body is unable to control blood sugar levels, many complications can arise, including obesity, constant hunger and food cravings, hypoglycemia, and even severe hypoglycemia or diabetic shock that can lead to loss of consciousness, which can be life threatening. Because coconut oil can supply needed energy without insulin, it helps slow down the absorption of sugars into the bloodstream. Coconut has a low glycemic index, and helps prevent blood sugar fluctuations. This balances the amount of sugar that enters the bloodstream with the amount of insulin produced, helping reverse insulin resistance and improve glucose control. Taking 2–3 tablespoons of coconut oil can lower blood sugar levels that are 80–100 points above normal within half an hour, reducing cravings and improving energy levels.

Blood Circulation and Neuropathy

Good circulation is critical for diabetics, especially if you are experiencing numbness in your feet. Many diabetics get infections or cuts on their feet and don't realize it until it is too late. If this happens, serious complications can arise. Coconut oil is very beneficial for improving blood circulation and preventing or even reversing problems with lack of feeling in the feet and legs. Eating 2–3 tablespoons of coconut oil daily can reduce or even reverse poor circulation and return feeling to the affected area in as little as ten days. Eating coconut oil every day can also help reduce or eliminate diabetic neuropathy or nerve pain and tingling that occurs in the extremities.

CHAPTER 6

Immunity

One of the most interesting things about coconut is the way it is processed by the body. Once coconut enters the liver and is dispersed throughout the body as energy, the lauric acid in coconut oil is converted to monolaurin, which is the same fatty acid that babies make from the lauric acid in their mothers' milk. This same monolaurin is a powerful antibacterial that can prevent bacterial and protozoan infections, and can destroy viruses like measles and HIV.

A Coconut Secret Your Doctor Won't Tell You

When you are coughing and sneezing, you might ponder going to a medical doctor. Depending on who you end up seeing, you may walk out with an antibiotic or you may end up with nothing in hand because you most likely have a virus. Viruses can be deadly, but instead of doing nothing, what if you could go home to your pantry and give your body a little help? This may be one of the most important chapters you read if you want to stay healthy or if you get ill easily. Vibrant health is yours for the taking with the addition of coconut oil to your diet.

This might be revolutionary news, and you might be thinking, "Why don't doctors tell you this stuff?" That is a good question. Is this a new medical breakthrough? Is it so new that it hasn't caught on yet? The sad truth is that this is old knowledge. The original work was done by Dr. Jon Kabara in 1966. He figured out that certain medium-chain fatty acids (lauric acids) in coconut oil actually kill some viruses. He was looking for better ways to preserve food.

Dr. Kabara said, "Never before in the history of man is it so important to emphasize the value of lauric oils." The medium-chain fats in coconut oil are similar to fats in mother's milk and have similar nutriceutical effects. These health effects were recognized centuries ago in Ayurvedic medicine. Modern research has now found a common link between these two natural health products—their fat or lipid content. The medium-chain fatty acids and monoglycerides found primarily in coconut oil and mother's milk have miraculous healing power.

So why haven't you heard this amazing news from your doctor? Think about it. How bad would it make your doctor look if in one breath he told you to eat a low-fat diet and in the next breath he told you, "Go ahead and eat coconut oil every day so you stay healthy." It's not going to happen. The medical profession is married to the low-fat diet, and recommending fat for health would undermine more than fifty years of advice. Whether your doctor knows the power of coconut oil or not is irrelevant; you are ultimately the one who chooses what you eat.

Composition of Coconut Oil

Coconut oil is primarily composed of medium-chain fatty acids that have the ability to be absorbed by the cells without the need for insulin or enzymes.

The way that it is delivered to the body gives coconut oil the unique ability to fight systemic infections like *Candida albicans* and viral infections. In 1978, Jon Kabara found that MCFAs from coconut oil had the ability to kill bacteria, yeast, fungi, and enveloped viruses, or viruses that are enveloped in a membrane made up of lipids. Another MCFA in coconut oil is caprylic acid. The combination of caprylic acid and lauric acid kills bacteria, viruses, and fungi by causing their cell walls to disintegrate. What a powerful combination for immunity to disease!

Coconut Oil Versus Antivirals

Unlike standard antiviral medications that attack a virus's genetic material, the MCFAs in coconut oil work together to disintegrate viruses in a more natural way that has no side effects. Because coconut oil is similar in composition to the fatty acids in the virus's coating, the MCFAs are absorbed by the virus, thereby weakening the lipid membrane until it simply breaks apart. Not even the most resistant viruses are able to defend themselves against the power of coconut oil.

FACT

"Coconut oil supports the immune system by ridding the body of harmful microoganisms, thus relieving stress on the body."
—"Chronic Fatigue Syndrome," Bruce Fife, ND, *www.conuq.com*.

Coconut has been recognized as a healing food by indigenous cultures that have used the coconut as a traditional food for thousands of years. How does coconut oil help the body's immune system? In his article "Coconut Oil and Medium-Chain Triglycerides" from website *www.coconutresearchcenter.org*, Dr. Bruce Fife, a leading researcher on coconut and its effects on the body, explains the immunity properties of coconut:

Besides increasing your energy level, there are other very important benefits that result from boosting your metabolic rate: it (coconut oil) helps protect you from illness and speeds healing. When metabolism is increased, cells function at a higher rate of efficiency. They heal injuries quicker, old and diseased cells are replaced faster, and young, new cells are generated at an increased rate to replace worn-out ones. Even the immune system functions better.

Coconut oil, simply by boosting the metabolic rate, has solved several problems with one solution: Boosting the immune system protects against diseases like type 2 diabetes, thyroid disorders, inflammatory diseases, and brain disease simply by allowing the cells in your body to proliferate and replace old cells faster. And, it kills the bacteria and viruses that make you sick. Where antibacterial medications are able to lessen the severity of an illness, coconut oil is able to not only kill viral infections and bacterial infections, it is able to build up your immune system and protect you from future infections, as well. After fifty years of research, properties in coconut oil have been found to be destructive to:

- Enveloped viruses, including HIV, herpes, cytomegalovirus, influenza, measles
- Pathogenic bacteria, *Listeria monocytogenes*, *Helicobacter pylori*, chlamydia, *Staphylococcus aureus*, *Staphylococcus agalactiae*, groups A, F, and G streptococci, gram-positive organisms
- Protozoa, including giardia lamblia
- Fungi, including several species of ringworm
- Yeast, including *Candida albicans*

That's an impressive list, especially for something that grows from a palm tree. The power of nature is something to appreciate and respect. The humble coconut contains some impressive fats.

Coconut Oil and Viruses

Monolaurin, the powerful antiviral that is produced when the body processes coconut oil, is the same monolaurin that protects babies from illness and disease when they are fed their mother's milk. Monolaurin has been shown in studies to be able to slow the progress of HIV and is effective in helping fight herpes, Epstein-Barr, and influenza.

Coconut Oil and Bacteria

A great example to show how coconut oil battles bacteria is its effect on the bacteria that causes pneumonia. Monolaurin is effective in speeding recovery from pneumonia. In a small research study conducted at the Philippine Children's Medical Center in Quezon City, forty children between the ages of three months and five years old who were given coconut oil recovered almost sixteen hours (15.6) sooner than the children who weren't.

Coconut Oil and Fungal Infections

Coconut oil is effective for treating ringworm, athlete's foot, and foot and toenail fungus. The caprylic acid in coconut oil is the component of coconut oil that has been shown to fight fungus. It is so effective that supplement manufacturers have used it in products designed to fight systemic yeast infections like candida.

FACT

Dr. Mary Enig, PhD, one of the world's leading authorities on fat, stated that monolaurin, a component of coconut oil, is the antiviral, antibacterial, and antiprotozoal monoglyceride used by the body to destroy lipid-coated viruses such as HIV, herpes, cytomegalovirus, and influenza, as well as pathogenic bacteria like *Listeria monocytogenes* and *Helicobacter pylori*, and protozoa such as *Giardia lamblia*.

Candida is a yeast infection out of control that can be caused by an imbalance of bacteria in the body. If you have ever been on antibiotics, there is a good chance that you have some yeast overgrowth. When the antibiotics kill the bacteria that caused your illness, they also wiped out all of the good bacteria, as well. This allows the naturally occurring yeasts in your body, which are usually kept in check by beneficial bacteria, to grow unchecked. Coconut oil has the ability to kill these yeasts and help restore the balance of bacteria in the body. If you have candida, you should also be taking probiotics with the coconut oil to help build up the good bacteria in your digestive tract. Things that can help build up these beneficial bacteria are kefir, yogurt, and probiotic supplements that you can find at your health food store.

Coconut Oil and Protozoan Parasite Infections

If you have ever had a protozoan infection like giardia, you understand how miserable these can be. If gone untreated, these infections can last for months and even lead to dehydration and kidney failure. Protozoan infections are often spread through unclean water sources, but in many developing countries where coconut is eaten on a regular basis, populations do not suffer from these infections, even when they drink contaminated water. This is because of the antimicrobial lipids found in coconut, which are so powerful in protecting from disease.

Coconut Oil and Vitamin Absorption

Coconut oil also helps boost immunity by helping your body absorb fat-soluble vitamins like A, D, E, and K and minerals like iron, calcium, and magnesium. These vitamins are critical to a strong immune system and strong bones. Without healthy fats in the diet, your body is unable to absorb these vitamins and minerals. When a diet is high in unsaturated fats like soy and canola oils, vitamin D cannot be absorbed, which is why after rickets was eradicated through improved diet we are now beginning to see cases of the disease. If only we could say the same about the common cold! With proper absorption of these critical vitamins through the daily use of healthy saturated fats, we could all but eliminate colds and flu.

ALERT

Research done at the University at Buffalo on fats and the immune system found that runners who severely limited fat intake may be seriously compromising their immunity to disease and lowering their body's resistance to inflammation. Results between two groups of runners showed that those who ate a diet high in fat had twice as many leukocytes, the body's top defense against infection. Runners who ate the low-fat diet had increased levels of the prostaglandins that cause inflammation.

Building Natural Immunity

With a proper diet that includes enough saturated fat, the body is able to build natural immunity to disease. Our society is so caught up in the idea of science preventing illness and research for new cures that perhaps we have overlooked the strongest source of natural immunity available—our own food! By demonizing fats, we are possibly self-sabotaging our own health. Saturated fat, especially the medium-chain fatty acids found in coconut oil, are essential to the body to maintain health and a strong immune system.

Healthy fats help the body build up the leukocytes that produce antibodies and help fight off infection and disease. Coconut oil not only aids in the production of these leukocytes, it has its own powerful disease-fighting mechanism that enhances the body's natural immune system, working with the antibodies to fight viruses, bacteria, and fungal infections.

Coconut Oil and Cancer

Coconut oil also has anticarcinogenic effects, meaning that it has the ability to kill cancer cells. In a study conducted by the Division of Nutritional Carcinogenesis, American Health Foundation, published by Bandaru S. Reddy, PhD, in *Dietary Fat and Colon Cancer: Animal Model Studies*, a group of rats had been chemically induced to have colon cancer. One group of rats was fed food with coconut oil while others had other dietary oils added to their food, including olive oil, corn oil, and safflower oil. The rats fed olive oil had fewer cancers develop, and the rats given food with coconut oil did not develop cancer.

This strong healing power in coconut oil is likely due to the way that it inserts itself into the cells, increasing metabolism and causing healthy cells to grow at a faster rate. When the body has the appropriate building blocks to form on the cellular level, things just seem to fall into place naturally.

CHAPTER 7

Eat Your Beauty Treatment

Coconut oil is not only good for you, it is probably one of the world's best beauty treatments! In spite of the large number of skin creams, hydrating serums, and moisturizing lotions available on the market, the best beauty treatments are the ones that you take in to your body. Healthy foods give your body what it needs to build beautiful skin, hair, and nails. This does not mean that there is no value to applying moisturizers externally; in fact, coconut oil applied to the skin is a great moisturizer and helps protect your skin against sunburn. However, cell membranes are mostly made up of lipids, which are fats. Not just any fats, though. Cell membranes are made of about 50 percent saturated fats. And the only really effective way to get those saturated fats permanently into your system in a way that will greatly improve skin tone and reduce dryness is to eat them.

How Can Coconut Oil Help?

Coconut oil is anti-inflammatory. It also has antifungal qualities. Eating coconut oil can act as a beauty treatment that works from the inside out by:

- Improving skin tone
- Reducing the appearance of wrinkles
- Improving itchy, dry skin
- Healing acne
- Reducing the appearance of stretch marks
- Adding shine to your hair
- Restoring flexibility and shine to dry, brittle nails
- Firming up soft, flabby muscles
- Accelerating weight loss
- Reducing cellulite
- Helping remineralize tooth enamel
- Helping to whiten stained teeth
- Eliminating bad breath
- Improving the smell of stinky feet
- Helping with unpleasant body odor
- Relieving dandruff from a dry, flaky scalp
- Helping to reduce calluses on your feet
- Getting rid of unsightly yellow toenail fungus
- Helping to get rid of athlete's foot

Skin

Coconut oil helps reduce dry skin and heal acne because when you eat the coconut oil, your body transports the oil directly to the parts of your body that need hydration. Rather than being oily, your skin will have the building blocks that it needs to naturally stop drying out as fast. When your body does not have the needed lipids or saturated fat to form the lipids that make up your cell membranes, your skin cells dry out and die at a faster rate.

Part of what causes acne is that dead skin blocks pores, and the natural oils in your skin become trapped and get infected. Properly hydrated skin that has the needed amount of fat to form healthy cell membranes and maintain proper hydration of surface skin cells does not dry out as fast, and dead cells do not get stuck on your skin, but slough off naturally as the body was designed to do. This prevents pores from becoming plugged, and prevents dirt and other impurities from becoming trapped where infection can occur. Also, properly hydrated skin that is firm with natural elasticity is much less likely to form wrinkles and stretch marks.

Hair and Nails

Dull hair and flaky, brittle nails, like dry skin, are caused by a lack of the proper building blocks for your body to continue to grow strong, shiny hair and flexible nails that have a healthy sheen. Without saturated fat, your nails and hair will be dull and brittle. By eating 2 tablespoons of coconut oil daily, you should notice a difference within three to five days.

FACT

Coconut oil has been used for thousands of years in many cultures to promote beauty. Coconut is high in fatty acids that boost the immune system and slow the aging process.

You can also get great results with topical applications of coconut oil—just warm the oil and rub it into your scalp. Allow it to soak for about thirty minutes before washing. Shampoo and rinse with warm water—not hot—so that you don't rinse off all of the oils that you have just added to your scalp. Rub the warmed oil into your skin and nails, as well, for a moisturizer that will bring a healthy glow. Topical application of coconut oil is very effective short term; however, a word of warning! If you want longer-lasting, more permanent results, it really works best if you are also eating the coconut oil on a daily basis.

Muscle Tone

Flabby muscles that can't seem to firm up no matter how hard your work them is a sign that your cell membranes are not made of a strong enough material. If you build a wall out of water balloons, it will sag and be unable to fulfill its purpose. This is the same idea with your muscles. If you build the cell membranes with trans fats and too many liquid oils that are naturally unstable and high in omega-6, the cell membranes will be saggy. A muscle made of saggy cells will not have the firm muscle tone that will give you the firm toned look that is part of a strong, beautiful physique. Not only that, but weak cell membranes lack the ability to block out viruses and other harmful substances that will make you sick.

Cellulite

Bumpy stores of fat beneath the surface of the skin that you can't seem to shake off are the dreaded curse known as cellulite. Eating coconut oil daily can help reduce cellulite by giving your body the key it needs to unlock and wash those excess fat stores out of your body. The body needs certain fatty acids in order to allow it to metabolize fat stores. The medium-chain fatty acids and the lauric acid in coconut oil act as a key that allows your body to let go of unneeded fat stores by reducing inflammation and boosting your metabolism, burning off the coconut oil you just ate and additional fat stores, as well. Eating coconut oil also makes the skin softer, smoother, and more elastic, so that the appearance of cellulite is naturally reduced over time.

Teeth and Dental Hygiene

Certain vitamins and minerals cannot be absorbed by your body without fat. You can eat as many greens as you like or drink as much milk as you like or even take scads of calcium supplements, but your body will not be able to properly utilize the calcium in these foods unless it has enough fat to help your body process it. It is the same with fat-soluble vitamins such as A and D, both of which are essential for the formation of strong bones and healthy teeth. If absorbed in the right balance, these vitamins can even help heal cavities and aid in the remineralization of tooth enamel. Coconut's natural antifungal and antibacterial properties also help with reducing tooth decay by inhibiting the growth of bacteria in your mouth. This, along with your body's natural remineralization process, helps build thicker enamel, and as a result, you will have a whiter, brighter smile.

Rinsing with coconut oil for 15 minutes 2–3 times a week will help with descaling and naturally whitening teeth. This rinsing process, called oil pulling, should be done by taking a tablespoon of melted coconut oil in your mouth and gently sucking and swishing it around in your mouth and between your teeth continually for 15 minutes. When done, spit out the oil because it actually removes toxins from your body—so you won't want to swallow it! After rinsing, brush your teeth as usual. You will notice whiter teeth and healthier gums after about two weeks.

Fungal Infections

Using coconut oil topically for conditions like callused feet, a dry itchy scalp, and toenail fungus can be very effective, as long as you continue the treatment, because coconut oil has antifungal properties that help fight fungal infections. Unpleasant body odors can also be caused by an internal fungal infection called candida. If you have trouble with chronic fungal infections, this is a sign that you probably have candida overgrowth. Candida is an internal yeast or fungal infection that sets in throughout your system, wreaking havoc with every bodily function. Because of its antifungal properties, eating coconut oil daily can help eliminate candida and restore your natural beauty.

Free Radicals

Brown patches, uneven skin tone, freckle-like spots, and wrinkles are signs of free-radical damage attributed to exposure to the sun. However, what most people don't understand is that our bodies have adapted over thousands of years to survive even in extreme sun exposure. In parts of the world where people wore little to no clothing, when they ate traditional diets, even the elderly in their populations did not exhibit the kind of free-radical damage that we do now.

Free radicals cause cellular degeneration over time, as atoms in cells lose electrons and then become unstable because of the remaining unpaired electrons. Basically, the cell begins to oxidize. Antioxidants are able to prevent this oxidization and stabilize the unpaired electrons by supplying an additional electron, and thereby slowing the aging process.

Free-radical damage is not limited to the fair skinned—all people experience aging skin. The good news is that there are things that you can do to reduce and even repair free radical damage. Most free-radical damage is caused by unhealthy fats in your diet. Trans fats and unhealthy vegetable oils reduce your skin's ability to withstand exposure to the sun, because each of your cell membranes is made up of fats or lipids. When you eat unhealthy oils and trans fats, your cells have no choice but to build those cells from lower quality building blocks, and this creates skin cells that are less resistant to damage from the environment.

Coconut oil acts as a natural sunscreen. Using coconut oil on your skin will help your skin tan more deeply and it will help your skin retain moisture, preventing peeling that is caused from dry skin.

This explains why indigenous peoples in tropical climates who ate traditional foods, including coconut oil, and who rarely wore clothing did not get skin cancer or free-radical damage. We can rebuild our body's natural defenses against free-radical damage by improving our diets and going back to natural, unprocessed, whole foods and by replacing margarine, shortening, and unstable vegetable oils like corn and soy oil with healthy fats like coconut oil, butter, olive oil, and rendered animal fats. Coconut oil is especially beneficial for preventing this free-radical damage. Its medium-chain fatty acid structure, which is very stable, prevents it from oxidizing or going rancid, and it contains a high level of antioxidants that are able to counteract the effect of free radicals on your body.

Ultraviolet Radiation

As you age, your skin naturally loses elasticity and is also less able to heal, as it is constantly exposed to the ultraviolet (UV) rays of the sun. UV rays accelerate damage caused by free radicals, but eating coconut oil and applying it directly to your skin can help reduce or prevent this damage. Unrefined coconut oil is very powerful and can help your body build a natural defense against UV rays.

Rubbing coconut oil on your skin can also offer protection from sunburns, but don't slather yourself in coconut oil and go out in direct sunlight for several hours if you are very fair skinned and have not been in direct exposure to the sun in a long time. You have to give your skin time to build up resistance to burning. Continue eating coconut oil each day and applying coconut oil to your skin, and build up resistance to sunburns by only allowing a short amount of sun exposure each day until you have built up enough resistance to be in the sun for a reasonable amount of time. If you feel like you are beginning to burn, move out of direct sunlight!

CHAPTER 8

Energy and Athletic Performance

A lack of energy can put the brakes on your hopes and dreams by magnifying molehills and turning them into mountains. Chronic fatigue and other conditions that sap your energy are real, and at times just getting out of bed in the morning feels like an insurmountable task. To make matters worse, turning to coffee and caffeine just adds the chains of addiction and the increased risk of high blood pressure and other damaging side effects to an already difficult problem.

Fueling the Fire

There is a nonaddictive solution to lack of energy! But coconut oil isn't a quick fix to all energy problems. Coconut needs to be added to your regular lifestyle and consumed on a daily basis to get lasting results. The reason that coconut can increase energy levels has to do with the way coconut oil is used by the body.

Coconut Oil and Digestion

Normally, when a person eats saturated fats, those fats, with their long-chain fatty acids (LCFAs), are broken down into their various individual fatty acids with help from enzymes produced by the pancreas. These fatty acids are then stored in the liver until the body runs out of energy from carbohydrate intake. Since most people have diets that are very high in carbohydrates, this could take quite some time, since most of the carbohydrates that are being consumed are not being used, but are instead converted to fat and stored in the body's adipose tissue. And, if your metabolism is slow, it will take even longer. Not only is it going to take longer to burn the fat you just ate, it is going to be nearly impossible to burn the excess carbs that have been tucked away into the body's fat stores for later.

A slow metabolism contributes to fatigue, so increasing the metabolism is very beneficial for those with low energy levels. This can be helped significantly by adding coconut oil to the diet. Coconut oil is unique in that its medium-chain fatty acids are used immediately for energy.

MCFAs and Energy

MCFAs are part of what makes coconut oil so unique. MCFAs are taken into the liver and absorbed immediately into the body. They do not need enzymes to be broken down, and they can be dissolved into the bloodstream. Therefore, they are able to be absorbed by cells and used as energy immediately! This allows your pancreas to rest, which is important, especially if you have adrenal fatigue or hypothyroid disorder, conditions that cause fatigue. It is important to be able to rest your adrenals so that they can heal and get back to full production levels. Once taken into the liver, instead of going through the rest of the standard digestive process, coconut oil is converted directly into energy through a process called thermogenesis. When coconut oil is eaten on a regular, daily basis, it increases your metabolism and produces energy that can help you get through the day without dragging.

FACT

In a study published in the *Journal of Nutrition*, mice were given an endurance test of having to swim against a current. Over a six-week period, some mice were fed a diet high in MCFAs while others were not. The study conclusively showed that the mice that were fed MCFAs had more endurance and could swim for longer periods of time against the current than the mice who had not been given MCFAs.

After these MCFAs are taken into the bloodstream, they have the ability to enter into the cells and be immediately used as energy. This is especially important to those who have conditions where the mind or body is unable to utilize glucose properly, like Alzheimer's disease and insulin-resistant diabetes. This can also help those who are able to use glucose by adding another route by which the body can get energy. This helps individuals who have chronic energy problems, since the nutrients in coconut oil are so readily available, allowing metabolism to increase and energy levels to rise.

Healing Fatigue Disorders

Most fatigue disorders can be linked to chronic infection, hypothyroidism, or low adrenal production in some way. Coconut oil is known to kill bacteria and yeast overgrowth and stimulate the thyroid. As a result, the related symptoms will subside. Coconut oil also allows the body to absorb more vitamin D and iron, both of which are critical for energy. The following outlines some of the problems that cause fatigue and how coconut oil can help.

Chronic Fatigue

Chronic fatigue can be caused by many things, but there is no one definitive cause. It is often caused by a low-grade chronic bacterial infection. These types of infections can be almost impossible to diagnose, and there is not a lot that medical science can do about them except administer antibiotics, which are often ineffective in the case of chronic fatigue.

Once it is in your system, coconut oil acts as an antibacterial and can eliminate low-level chronic infections. This effect, added to coconut oil's ability to effectively raise metabolism, can restore your depleted energy levels. Simply add coconut oil to your diet and eat it every day for a period of several months.

Thyroid Disease

If you have cold hands and feet, low body temperature, sensitivity to cold, dry skin, insomnia, hair loss, headaches, anxiety attacks, dizziness, loss of libido, brittle nails, constipation, brain fog, a hoarse voice, ringing in the ears, puffy eyes, are susceptible to frequent infections, are always tired, and/or have seemingly uncontrollable weight gain, you might have a thyroid disorder. Thyroid disorders, especially borderline thyroid disorders, can be difficult to diagnose, especially if your doctor is not willing to do a full thyroid panel. Coconut oil can raise the basal body temperature and support the thyroid. Often, low thyroid function can be reversed by removing unstable vegetable oils from the diet and replacing them with coconut oil.

Anemia

Coconut is a great source of vitamins and iron. The fatty acids in the coconut oil help your body to absorb vitamins and minerals and can thereby effectively prevent anemia. One cup of shredded coconut contains almost 2 milligrams of iron.

Food Allergies

Another common cause of fatigue is food sensitivities or allergies. Allergies to coconut are rare, and since coconut can be used in many different ways, it can be a good substitute for high-allergy foods. Another reason that allergies can cause fatigue is because of inflammation. Coconut oil is an anti-inflammatory and can help reduce symptoms of allergies.

Heart Disease

Heart disease constricts the arteries and can prevent the body from getting adequate amounts of oxygen, causing fatigue and shortness of breath. Coconut is beneficial to heart health and can even reverse or prevent heart disease.

Fibromyalgia

Symptoms of fibromyalgia include pain and swelling in your joints and muscles, migraine headaches, brain fog, poor concentration, depression, feeling stiff and sore in the morning on waking, sensitivity to cold, allergies, irritable bowel syndrome, insomnia and difficulty sleeping, muscle weakness, and chronic fatigue. Since fibromyalgia is an inflammatory disease, coconut oil, with its anti-inflammatory properties, can help a great deal with reducing symptoms within a month by using 3–4 tablespoons per day.

Boosting Athletic Performance with Coconut Oil

Coconut oil is not only great for healing, but for increasing stamina in already healthy individuals. Coconut oil is used by body builders, athletes, and even race horse trainers to increase energy and endurance. It provides means for quick weight loss for athletes who have to reach a certain weight for competition, provides long-lasting endurance for runners and swimmers, and works as a great postworkout fuel for the body to quickly restore energy and provide fast healing for the repetitive stress athletes are under as they push themselves to be stronger and faster.

Not only is coconut oil nonaddictive and free of nasty side effects, it really works. Intense and prolonged periods of physical exercise can weaken the immune system without proper fuel for the body. Carbohydrates can act as quick energy, but a healthy diet needs to have fat in order to function optimally. High-carb, low-fat diets can eventually wear a person down, and do not have the right building blocks to maintain long-lasting energy and endurance while helping the body rebuild damaged muscle tissue and joints. There are many reasons why athletes will want to consider making coconut and coconut oil a regular part of their diet.

FACT

There are many companies that sell coconut oil supplements for racing horses to increase endurance and speed as well as to promote overall health and well being. In Australia and the United Kingdom, race horse trainers often add coconut oil to their horse's feed. One coconut oil supplement, Race-Torque, claims to give your race horse a "pre-event energy boost."

Coconut Oil Is Fast Acting

Coconut oil is fast acting because it is quickly assimilated into the body for a quick source of energy.

Increases Endurance

Carb loading is still practiced by many athletes for quick energy before and after athletic events, but this idea is dangerous in the long run. The body needs fats—the brain, myelin sheath or protective coating of nerve cells, and individual cell membranes in all parts of the body are all made up of fats. If the body does not get enough fats, eventually, everything starts to break down. Carbs may give a quick burst of energy, but for long-lasting energy and endurance, the body needs fats. Coconut oil is an ideal fat for endurance because of the way that it is metabolized in the body, increasing metabolism and energy in a slow, even stream instead of in a burst.

Enhance Performance

Using coconut oil regularly enhances performance naturally, without the use of dangerous substances like drugs or steroids, by building up the body and preventing illness. Coconut oil provides the body with a ready-to-use energy source that doesn't run out, thereby increasing the body's ability to perform at its optimal level.

Speed Healing and Repair

Coconut oil has natural healing properties and has traditionally been used as a medicine in many cultures. It is often referred to as the tree of life because of its great capacity for healing. Adding coconut oil to your diet speeds healing of damage caused by prolonged physical exercise.

Ways to Add Coconut Oil to Your Diet

It is easy to add coconut oil to your diet—just substitute coconut oil wherever you would normally use other oils. Eliminate any hydrogenated fats and liquid vegetable oils from your diet, and always check labels to make sure they are not hidden in the foods that you are eating. There is no need to eliminate other healthy animal fats, but coconut oil should be used regularly for optimal results.

ALERT

Most liquid vegetable oils are unstable and unsuitable for cooking with, even "high smoke point" oils that are supposed to be safe for cooking with. Heating liquid vegetable oils that are high in omega-6 long-chain fatty acids causes them to go rancid and turns them into trans fats. Coconut oil is very stable and is perfectly safe for frying foods.

Cooking

Coconut oil is very stable and can be used for frying and cooking without causing rancidity. A major problem with other vegetable oils is that heating them causes them to go rancid, turning them into a hotbed of free radicals and toxic trans fats that can cause damage to your cellular structure and lead to type 2 diabetes and heart disease. Always read the label on your coconut oil to make sure it is not hydrogenated or even partially hydrogenated. For best results, it should also be cold-pressed virgin coconut oil.

Spreads

Coconut oil, coconut butter, and coconut cream can be made into delicious spreads for toast, to put on vegetables, and for eating with crackers.

Smoothies

For extra energy and a power-packed breakfast, add a tablespoon of coconut oil to a fruit smoothie. This will give you lasting energy and kick your cravings until lunch time.

Mix It In

Mix a tablespoon of coconut oil into hot cereal, yogurt, or rice.

By the Spoonful

Take coconut oil as a supplement simply by eating a spoonful in the morning along with breakfast.

As a Supplement

There are soft gel capsules that can be taken as a dietary supplement, but care should be taken to make sure that the oil in these is of the highest quality. It is easier to ensure high-quality coconut oil by using virgin coconut oil in your cooking and adding it to your food.

Can You Take Too Much?

As with any good thing, it is possible to take too much coconut oil. If you start to experience gastrointestinal discomfort, it would be a good idea to cut back. When starting to use coconut oil as a dietary supplement, it is best to start with a teaspoon and then increase the dosage until you can comfortably take 2–4 tablespoons spread throughout the day.

CHAPTER 9

Mental and Neurological Health

Coconut oil is a special saturated fat, unlike any other! The medium-chain fatty acids in coconut oil are unique in the way they are used by the body. When your body metabolizes long-chain fatty acids, it can either use them immediately as energy or store them as fat. MCFAs, however, which the body metabolizes into ketones, are soluble in the blood and cannot be easily stored as fat. They are one of the only energy sources that can be used directly for energy by the brain, and because of this they have some very amazing healing properties when it comes to brain function and mental illness.

How Does Coconut Oil Affect the Brain?

Coconut oil is constructed of medium-chain fatty acids called ketones, which have some amazing properties. Ketones are one of the only energy sources used by the brain. Normally, the brain uses glucose as an energy source for optimal brain function, and only uses ketones produced from your body's fat stores once there is no more available glucose. For this to happen, a person would have to be starving before any ketones were available as energy for the brain. The brain cannot use long-chain fatty acids—saturated fats found in animal foods—for energy the way the body can, because they cannot cross the blood-brain barrier. However, medium-chain fatty acids from coconut oil are able to cross the blood-brain barrier, and can be used by the brain as an energy source.

FACT

Ketones are water-soluble compounds that are created when the body metabolizes fat. They can be used as a source of energy by the heart and the brain. Ketone bodies are normally created in times of prolonged fasting or through metabolizing medium-chain fatty acids from coconut oil.

So what does this mean? It means that if the brain is no longer able to use glucose as an energy source, as in the case of brain diseases like Alzheimer's or dementia, these ketones can nourish the brain and prevent or even reverse some of the damage caused by the brain's inability to utilize glucose. In short, it means that if you are suffering from a degenerative brain disease, you may be able to slow or stop the degenerative process by eating a small amount of coconut oil every day!

Brain Fog

That fuzzy, kind-of-forgetful fog that seems to descend upon you when you are trying to remember where you put the keys, where you parked, or what you did over the past week has become known as "brain fog"—the feeling that you are forgetting things or that you are not thinking as clearly as you should be.

Brain fog is caused by slowing nerve impulses in the brain, where a synapse passes an electrical signal from one brain cell to another. A normal synapse passes in seventy-five microseconds, while in a person with dementia these synapses can take as long as 140 microseconds. When you have brain fog, your synapses are firing somewhere between those; the slower the synapse, the more foggy things become. Adding coconut oil to your diet can clear things up by providing a good source of saturated fat to remyelinate your nerves. This aids in speeding up the amount of time that nerve impulses travel from one cell to another, and provides additional energy to the brain for proper brain function.

FACT

In her book *Alzheimer's Disease: What If There Was a Cure? The Story of Ketones*, Dr. Mary Newport discusses how she discovered that coconut oil can help treat people with Alzheimer's disease. Her husband began falling deeper into dementia and could not qualify for treatment under an Alzheimer's study because his disease had progressed too far. She began researching, and discovered a study done on MCT oil, which she learned from her research was derived from coconut oil. After giving her husband coconut oil, he was able to make enough of a recovery to qualify for a research study he had previously failed to meet the qualifications for.

Alzheimer's Disease

The brain uses glucose primarily as a source of energy, but in Alzheimer's disease, the brain becomes unable to utilize glucose, resulting in parts of the brain basically dying from starvation. Ketone bodies in coconut oil are still able to be used by the brain as an alternate energy source, and as a result, prevent these sections of the brain from dying. Research conducted at the University of Toronto, published in *Brain Research* in 2008, found that dogs with age-related cognitive decline who were fed MCT oil (which was derived from coconut oil) were able to make significant improvements in a short amount of time.

Even though very little research has been done on this subject, there are many anecdotal evidences that coconut oil can have a profound impact on those suffering from Alzheimer's and degenerative brain diseases.

Coconut Oil and Other Brain and Nervous Disorders

There has also been a very limited amount of research showing benefits of coconut oil for many other mental illnesses and neurological disorders. Most of the evidence is purely anecdotal, based on testimony of those who have used coconut oil. If you browse the Internet, you can find thousands of testimonials from people who have significantly reduced their symptoms of brain disease and neurological disorders ranging from depression and bipolar disorder to autism spectrum disorder and demyelinating disorders like multiple sclerosis and Guillain-Barré syndrome.

The reason that coconut oil helps with these problems has mostly to do with the way nerve and brain cells function. The brain and the myelin sheath are made mostly of fats, so they depend on the correct balance of fats and other compounds. This balance allows them to send electrical impulses from one cell to the other to transmit information through the nervous system and to and from the brain for processing. It also remyelinates the nerve cells when the myelin, or the fatty protective outer covering of the nerve cells, breaks down. If a nerve cell does not have this protective coating of fat, it is unable to correctly process electrical impulses so it can send or deliver messages to and from the brain, making whatever bodily function it controls stop working properly.

The transmission of electric impulses from cell to cell requires that the body have the right balance of omega-3 fatty acids. Although coconut does not contain any omega-3 fatty acids, it helps the body utilize these EFAs, while trans fats like margarine, shortening, and unstable vegetable oils actually block the body from being able to use these EFAs effectively; coconut oil has the opposite effect. The following are some brain and nervous disorders and how they are helped using coconut oil:

- **Bipolar disorder:** Many people with bipolar disorder report that taking coconut oil along with fish oil helps to control manic episodes. The reason for this would be that while the fish oil contains the needed EFAs the body needs to heal, the body needs the saturated fats from the coconut oil to effectively use the EFAs in the fish oil.
- **Depression:** Coconut oil helps stabilize the thyroid. Depression is often caused by hypothyroid disorder, or not producing an adequate amount of thyroid hormone, so once the thyroid is stabilized, the depression goes away. This may not have any effect on depression that is not thyroid related.
- **ADD/ADHD:** ADD and ADHD are aggravated by using unhealthy fats like margarine and other hydrogenated oils. Corn oil and soy oil can also trigger behavior problems in children with ADD/ADHD who have food allergies. Switching to healthy fats like coconut oil and butter can make a big difference, because again, the body needs a healthy source of saturated fat to process the EFAs that help the body heal.
- **OCD:** Obsessive-compulsive disorder can be helped by adding a combination of healthy fats to the diet, including fish oil, coconut oil, and butter. OCD is another disorder that can be alleviated through a good source of EFAs, which coconut oil helps the body to use properly.
- **Anxiety:** Many people suffering from anxiety attacks reported relief from their symptoms after adding coconut oil to their diets. Again, this is probably related to the way that coconut oil helps the body effectively utilize EFAs.
- **Mood disorders:** Improving the diet by adding healthy fats like coconut oil, fish oil, and butter can help alleviate symptoms of mood disorders for the same reasons that coconut oil is effective in helping treat OCD and anxiety.
- **Schizophrenia:** Schizophrenia, a mental illness characterized by delusions, hallucinations, and bizarre behavior, can be helped by taking coconut oil for the same reasons that it helps those with bipolar and anxiety disorders. Recent data gathered showed that patients with schizophrenia are deficient in omega-3 EFAs, and positive outcomes are linked to balancing the levels of omega-3 with other EFAs in the body. Eliminating trans fats and using coconut oil

helps reduce inflammation and allows the body to make better use of EFAs.

- **Autism:** Autism spectrum disorder is the name for a wide range of complex neurological development disorders combined with digestive issues, and can manifest itself through a whole range of problems including social development and food allergies. Coconut oil can help not only with assimilation of omega-3 EFAs, but the antifungal properties of coconut oil also aid in digestion, which is an issue for those with ASD.

- **Multiple sclerosis:** Coconut oil balances lipids in the body and reduces inflammation. Multiple sclerosis is an inflammatory disease that causes demyelination of the nerves, which means the myelin sheath, or the protective fatty coating on nerve cells, begins to deteriorate. Many MS researchers warn about the use of any saturated fats for those who suffer from MS, but the paradox there is that the body cannot utilize essential fatty acids without saturated fat, and if the body cannot utilize omega-3s, it cannot heal. Because coconut oil helps reduce inflammation and helps the body utilize essential fatty acids, which are vital for remyelination, coconut oil can help reduce and possibly reverse the symptoms of MS.

- **Guillain-Barré syndrome:** Guillain-Barré syndrome (GBS) is very similar to MS in that the immune system attacks the myelin sheath on the nervous system, but its attack focuses on the peripheral nervous system; MS attacks the central nervous system. Coconut oil will help GBS in the same way and for the same reason as it helps those with MS.

- **Lou Gehrig's disease:** Lou Gehrig's disease, or amyotrophic lateral sclerosis (ALS), is a neurological disease that causes a progressive degeneration of nerve cells in the brain and the spinal cord, which control voluntary muscles. This results in increasing weakness and atrophy of the muscles, usually beginning in the extremities and then moving throughout the body, causing paralysis. There are anecdotal reports of people reversing the nerve damage caused by ALS, and it may work in much the same way that coconut oil helps reverse brain damage caused by Alzheimer's disease.

Seizures

Ketones have also been found to be beneficial for people who are suffering from epileptic seizures. In his book *The Ketogenic Diet: A Treatment for Children and Others with Epilepsy*, Dr. John M. Freeman outlines how children on a high-fat diet using MCT from coconut oil were able to significantly reduce the number of seizures they were having or eliminate them completely, in as little as five days.

The ketogenic diet is based on a diet developed in the early 1900s, which was successfully used to control seizures in children in the 1920s and 1930s. The diet was designed to mimic the metabolic state during starvation because when the body is in starvation mode, it depletes its store of glucose and begins to burn fat. This process produces ketones—the same thing produced when the body metabolizes coconut oil. These ketone bodies seem to have a suppressing effect on the seizures.

By feeding an epileptic child a diet so high in fats, there are no more carbohydrates to burn, so the body must burn fats for energy. This process produces ketones, which seem to have some kind of protective effect on the brain, helping to even out the electrical impulses in the brain that cause the seizures. Coconut oil, which is easily converted into ketones by the body, enhances this effect. Doctors admittedly do not know how or why the ketogenic diet works to control seizures, but it does work, and in many cases, it works just as well or in some cases better than seizure medications.

ALERT

Ketonic diets should not be attempted without guidance from a licensed health care professional. High-fat diets need to be optimally balanced to give the body a proper balance of omega-3s and other healthy fats. Using poor-quality fats to simply boost caloric intake will not have the same benefits, and would be dangerous to your health.

The ketogenic diet was developed by researchers who were studying the metabolic effect of diet on diabetics in the early 1900s. They noticed that a high-fat, low-carbohydrate diet produced metabolic conditions similar to starvation. Since the Middle Ages, fasting for long periods of time—drinking only water for between ten to twenty days—had been routinely used to control seizures with some success. When it was discovered that the same effect could be achieved through a high-fat diet, this technique began to be widely used but was forgotten once antispasmodic drugs were developed in 1938.

CHAPTER 10

Meal Planning

Meal planning can be a daunting task when you are already overwhelmed with the rush of daily life. Add bills, a picky spouse and/or children, pets, and health issues to the mix, and it can seem almost impossible to plan and prepare healthy meals. But by making a few simple changes using the information in this chapter, you will be able to create a meal-planning strategy that will work for your family.

How Can I Get Mealtime Under Control?

The best way to tame the mealtime madness is by establishing a routine. Some tools that you can use to make mealtimes more manageable are menus, make-ahead mixes, and taking a few minutes to plan meals once a week, with a major planning session once a month.

You can make several weekly menus that you can rotate to keep variety, and if you like you can write in a wild-card meal where you can either leave a space for an evening out or room for a spontaneous meal choice. Whatever you do, try to get the family's input so that the whole house doesn't rebel against you—good food is expensive, and being proactive this way will help avoid a lot of unnecessary waste.

Plan three meals a day plus at least two healthy snacks. Once you have planned out one week of daily menus, go through the list of meals and make a list of groceries that you will need to have on hand to prepare those meals. It is very helpful to have the recipes out along with your menu-planning sheet so that you can make sure you have all the necessary ingredients.

Creating a Balanced Meal

A balanced meal should have a variety of foods, including fats, carbohydrates, proteins, and small amounts of natural sweets. Sweets and simple carbohydrates need to be balanced with healthy fats to prevent blood sugar spikes that signal your body to begin producing insulin that will capture those simple sugars in your bloodstream and convert them to fat. Nuts, grains, and seeds should be whole, and they should be soaked overnight in water with a little lemon juice or whey to break down the phytic acids that will prevent your body from accessing the nutrients in the grains. The American diet tends to be very heavy on the grains, but a good balanced meal will contain a variety of foods from animal foods, grains, legumes, nuts, fruits and vegetables, and healthy fats and oils. More important than the number of calories consumed is the balance of a variety of foods, and that the foods are whole and chosen from clean, organic food sources.

According to the United States Department of Agriculture ChooseMy Plate (*www.choosemyplate.gov*), a balanced meal consists of half fruits and vegetables, a little more than ¼ grains, and a little less than ¼ protein, with a small side of dairy. They recommend that half of your grains should be whole grains, which conversely means that it is okay if a little over ⅛ of every meal is made up of processed grains. None of the food groups makes mention of any fats, and in the link to information about fats and oils, there is no distinction made between hydrogenated fats and fats that are naturally solid at room temperature. The USDA states: "Oils are generally better for your health than solid fats because they contain less saturated fats and/or trans fats." There are no mentions of any positive effects of natural saturated fats like coconut oil, even though there is plenty of research available that shows the benefit of saturated fats in the diet and the inflammatory properties of these "healthy" oils.

FACT

Traditional diets consisted of a much higher intake of fats than we eat now. The USDA food pyramid recommends a very low percentage of fat—between 20 and 30 percent—which is very unhealthy, especially when combined with a diet that is very high in carbohydrates.

As many of us battle health issues caused directly by following recommendations, it can be very confusing when adhering to this dietary advice if it makes us fat and sick. So how do we determine what a balanced meal is?

Cut Out the Junk

A few simple guidelines would be to start by cutting out any processed foods, especially refined sugars and grains. Cut out all processed fats and replace refined table salt with unrefined sea salt. All solid fats should be naturally solid at room temperature.

Grains

If you eat grains, make them soaked whole grains and only about ⅛ of your plate, if at all. You can mix grains with nuts and legumes such as lentils or beans to make up a little less than ¼ of your plate. Alternate grains with starchy foods like potatoes with the skins, plantains, or a variety of legumes, which can make up a little less than ¼ of your plate. When you do eat grains, mix them up. Most people only eat rice and wheat. There are many others to choose from; for example, quinoa makes a great side dish, and is not really a grain, but a starchy seed. Other seeds that you can add to your diet are chia, buckwheat, and flaxseed. On days that you eat grain, try a spelt or barley pilaf mixture with lentils, nuts, and seeds or a mixture of a variety of different types of rice.

Meats and Protein

Make a little less than ¼ of your plate a main-dish high-quality protein like wild-caught fish, pastured lamb, grass-fed beef, free-range poultry, or other meats. Meats need to be high quality—if we are what we eat, then it stands to reason that animals are what they eat, as well. Animals that have been fed poor-quality food will be poor-quality food. Leave the natural fat on the meat. Pastured lamb and grass-fed beef are naturally lower in fat than feedlot beef or their CAFO (concentrated animal feeding operations) counterparts. And the fat on naturally raised animals is not full of stored toxins like it is with animals who have been fed an unnatural diet under stressful living conditions. These fats are natural and healthy, and will work with the coconut oil to build strong pathogen-resistant cell membranes that will build stronger, more supple skin, firmer muscles, and minds that think more clearly.

Fruits and Vegetables

The one thing that the USDA probably got right was the fruits and vegetables. A little less than half of your plate should be fruits and vegetables. Choose a wide variety of fruits and vegetables in season. Eat a variety of colors and a variety of cooked and raw fruits and vegetables. When cooking vegetables, be careful not to overcook them! Vegetables should not be mushy—this destroys most of the nutritional value. Many vegetables can be eaten raw, but there are some vegetables that should be cooked to get the most nutrients out of them. These are the cruciferous or goitrogen vegetables like spinach, kale, broccoli, cabbage, and cauliflower.

Cruciferous or goitrogen vegetables contain thyroid-suppressing compounds that are broken down by cooking. It is unnecessary to cook them until they are mushy—a light steaming should do just fine. If you want to eat all of your food raw, then it may be better for you to skip goitrogen vegetables if you have thyroid problems.

Fats

The key part that the USDA guidelines leave out may be one of the most important components of a balanced meal, and that is the fats. Not only is every single cell in your body made up with a significant amount of fats, your brain is almost completely made of fat. Your vital organs—your heart, liver, and lungs—are cushioned with a thin layer of fat. Fats in your diet allow your body to be flexible, your skin to be soft and elastic, your hair and nails to be silky and smooth. Leaving out the fats is an unfortunate oversight, as it is one of the keys to vitality and good health. The little slice on your plate that you made room for by moving all of the other food groups over a bit should go toward your healthy fats. This section represents the 40–50 percent of your caloric intake from fats.

This idea of the plate is not exactly right, because fats are so much higher in calories than other foods that they really take up a lot less space than that—this space would represent the 1 tablespoon of butter you put on your vegetables, the fat on your meat, and a tablespoon of coconut oil that you might be adding as a dietary supplement. For example, if your meal was about 650 calories, about 3 tablespoons of fat goes in the empty slot and represents 46 percent of the calories from that meal. That gives you about 3 ounces of grass-fed beef with the fat, a ¾-cup serving of quinoa with coconut oil and salt, ½ cup sliced strawberries, and 1 cup of steamed asparagus with butter and salt.

Planning Ahead

Another aspect of meal planning is time. One thing that traditional cooking has against it is that it tends to be prohibitive when it comes to time. Let's face it—our lifestyle has changed considerably since the Paleolithic time period. Even over the last fifty years, our lives have become more and more packed with stuff. And this stuff is not always something that we can get away from. As much as we may want to tell our boss to stuff it, we still need to pay the electric bill. It is a good idea to simplify as much as possible, but at the same time, there are a few things that you can do to save time. You can prepare staple ingredients ahead of time. If you want to use fresh coconut milk, buy coconuts on sale and make up your coconut milk, shredded coconut meat, and other coconut products ahead of time and keep them in your freezer. If you don't have a freezer, you may want to consider having one. A freezer is a huge time saver when you are cooking traditional foods, because it allows you to keep frozen goods on hand that can be used in many recipes.

Making Mixes

Another time saver that can help is making mixes. You can make flour blends for use in baking, curry pastes for seasoning, or even precook meats and keep them in the freezer for use in recipes later.

ALERT

Nuts, grains, and seeds contain phytic acid, an acid that prevents the seed from sprouting before it is time. Unfortunately, this phytic acid also prevents your body form absorbing minerals and nutrients from these nuts, grains, and seeds as well as you would otherwise be able to. In fact, the phytic acid can actually cause mineral deficiencies in many people. Soaking nuts, grains, and seeds helps break down the phytic acid and unlocks nutrients in them, making them more bioavailable.

Presoaking Grains and Seeds

Grains and seeds can be soaked and either frozen or dehydrated for later use. If you plan on dehydrating nuts, grains, and seeds ahead of time and dehydrating them, you will want a good-quality large food dehydrator, or an oven that can be set as low as 100°F to 120°F.

Once they have been dehydrated, they can be stored in an airtight container, or grains and seeds can be ground ahead of time and stored for shorter periods of time.

Planning for Picky Eaters

Picky eaters are one of the most challenging parts about trying to make a change in your family's habits. If you have a child who will not even try new foods, changing your menu can be a real food fight! There are a few things that you can do to help the process along.

Do not cook separate meals. Cook one thing that everyone can eat. It will make things easier on you, and you will be able to spend less time cooking and more time with your family.

QUESTION

How can I avoid food fights with my children?
When it comes to planning meals, the last thing you want is a power struggle over food. A few tips to help avoid food fights are to give your child choices: Choose two or three things that you feel would be a healthy meal, and then let your child pick one. Let your child help you in the kitchen. Small children can help in small ways. Have a set dinner time—make sure your child gets fed before she gets cranky. Make sure that you give your child a small enough serving that she can eat it without getting too full, about 1 tablespoon of food per year of age.

Ease them into it. You may want to start with a familiar recipe that you know they like and make a few changes to it; for example, swap out unhealthy oils with coconut oil.

If they are extremely resistant to changes, start slowly. Allow your family to help choose the menu. You may want to help them go through several recipes and choose some that sound good to them.

Tell your family that you want to try some new recipes and that you want their help to know which ones they like and which ones they don't. Get them on board by making them into your official food testers. If they really don't like a recipe, discuss with them how you could change it to make it better, or decide as a group not to make it again. Mark your favorites and add them to a menu to have again another time.

Be firm. If you have a child who has food allergies and does not want to give up his or her favorite unhealthy foods, remember, you are the parent, and part of your job is to make sure that your child is healthy! They can't have it if you don't give it to them.

If it is your partner, realize that if you pressure him to change, it will only bring resentment. The best way to get an adult to change is by getting him onboard and through mutual cooperation. This is a lot easier to get if you are the one doing the cooking.

Eating on the Run

If you have a tight schedule that you can't change and find yourself eating on the run a lot, it can be really hard to get the proper nutrition that you need to stay healthy and energized throughout the day. Some things that you can do to help include the following:

- Make sure you have a blender and ingredients for your favorite smoothies on hand. Smoothies are a quick breakfast that can be carried with you. If you add chia seed and coconut oil, you will have a breakfast that has great staying power and gives you a lot of energy!
- Make lunches the night before that you can grab and take with you on the way out the door.
- Divide leftovers from the last meal and put them in individual serving containers marked with the date they were made, so that you can grab one and reheat it later.
- Make dressings and other recipes ahead of time so that they are ready when you need them.
- Go for quick, nutrient-dense foods that you can prepare ahead of time, or that require very little prep time. Adding coconut oil, for example, gives you energy and keeps you full longer.

ALERT

If you eat on the run, it is easy to miss meals or eat unhealthy fast foods. This leads to low energy and weight gain. A few things that you can do to counteract this are to add chia seed and coconut oil to your smoothies, add avocado to sandwiches and salads, and cut out the simple carbs like processed crackers or candy.

Quality Food on a Budget

Food is expensive, especially if you are trying to find the best-quality ingredients. When you have to have certain ingredients that are hard to find, because of food allergies or dietary restrictions, this can complicate things even more. There are a few things that you can do to save money and make your life a little easier in the process.

Find a local food co-op that will deliver to your neighborhood. Azure Standard is a food co-op group that has drop points in most states. If you do not have an available drop point in your area, you may be able to start one.

Make a list of websites that sell the items that you need, and then find one with the price that works best for you. Contact your local chapter of the Weston A. Price Foundation. Chapter leaders have access to local resources that can help you find the best prices for real food sources in your area.

ESSENTIAL

Shopping online can save you time and money. Some ways to save by shopping online are to take advantage of Amazon.com's free shipping on orders over $25 (make sure the purchase qualifies for free super saver shipping), join a food co-op like Azure Standard, or get a wholesale account at your favorite online coconut retailer and buy in bulk.

Remember that if you are going to start eating natural, organically grown food, if you buy from the store or the farmers market, you will pay more than you are used to paying for lower-quality food. Don't fret over it, just look over your budget and move some money from the medical category into your groceries category, because eating better-quality food means less money spent at the doctor's office.

Stay away from high-priced "organic" snack foods. Just because processed food is labeled organic doesn't really make it any better for you. High fructose corn syrup is still going to put you at risk for type 2 diabetes whether it is organic or not.

Look in your local classified ads and see if there is anyone selling fresh produce from their garden. Chances are they will not be charging as much as the farmers' market because they don't have the overhead that vendors there do.

Watch for sales. Some stores will have case-lot sales at least once a year.

Coupons are less relevant when you are buying real food because the coupons available are not usually for the things you are going to want; however, sometimes you can find good deals and generic coupons that can be used on anything that you want at a particular store. If you want to use coupons, PinchingYourPennies.com can make it easier for you to find the best deals by matching your coupons up to sale items in grocery stores in your area.

CHAPTER 11

Breakfast and Brunch

Fluffy Coconut Pancakes and Waffles

If you have gone gluten free, one of the things you may miss is a good pancake breakfast. These pancakes are gluten free, and go great with fresh fruit!

INGREDIENTS | MAKES 8 PANCAKES

3 eggs
¾ cup coconut milk
2 teaspoons coconut sugar
½ teaspoon sea salt
3 tablespoons virgin coconut oil, melted
½ cup coconut flour, sifted
1 teaspoon baking powder

1. Mix eggs, coconut milk, sugar, salt, and 2 tablespoons of coconut oil in a large bowl.

2. Thoroughly combine coconut flour and baking powder; mix into batter. Mixture will be thin at first, but as you stir, the coconut flour absorbs the liquid and the batter thickens. The batter will be thick, and will flatten out as the pancakes cook.

3. In a heavy-bottomed skillet, melt the remaining tablespoon of coconut oil.

4. Scoop batter onto skillet at medium heat, using ¼ cup measuring cup for each pancake.

5. Cook for about 1 minute, then turn. Cook for another minute, or until pancakes are cooked through and golden brown.

6. For waffles, scoop batter into a well-oiled waffle iron and follow cooking directions. Serve with Coconut Pancake Syrup (see recipe in this chapter).

PER 1 PANCAKE Calories: 146 | Fat: 12g | Protein: 4g | Sodium: 234mg | Fiber: 3g | Carbohydrates: 7g

Hawaiian Sunrise Green Smoothie

Looking for something fast? Green smoothies are a great way to get a nutrient-packed breakfast on the run.

INGREDIENTS | SERVES 6

1 banana, peeled

1 ripe mango, peeled and pitted

1 cup lightly steamed spinach leaves, cooled

½ ripe avocado, peeled and pitted

½ cup orange juice with pulp

½ cup coconut milk

1 tablespoon coconut oil

1. Blend all ingredients in a blender until smooth.

2. Divide among 6 glasses, and serve.

PER SERVING Calories: 138 | Fat: 9g | Protein: 2g | Sodium: 22mg | Fiber: 3g | Carbohydrates: 15g

Green Smoothies

Greens are packed with minerals; however, most greens are goitrogens and can suppress thyroid function when eaten raw. Lightly steaming greens, just until wilted, before eating them breaks down the compounds that cause this problem. To make using steamed greens easier, steam a few pounds at a time and then purée them in your blender. Scoop puréed spinach into ice cube trays and freeze for later use. Spinach cubes can be stored in a resealable plastic bag in your freezer. Add 1 or 2 cubes to your smoothie in place of every cup called for.

Fruit and Coconut Parfait

*These parfaits are a pretty way to get a nutrient-dense breakfast. Chia seed
is extremely filling, and is a great way to boost your energy!*

INGREDIENTS | SERVES 6

6 tablespoons chia seeds

4½ cups coconut yogurt

1½ cups chopped walnuts

¾ cup flaxseed

6 bananas, peeled

3 cups fresh mixed berries, plus 6
additional berries for garnish

Soaking Nuts, Grains, and Seeds

Nuts, grains, and seeds are high in phytates, an acid that prevents the seed from sprouting before the plant is ready to grow. Phytates can prevent you from being able to use the vitamins and minerals that are locked away in these nutrient-dense foods. To break down the phytates and make these nutrients available to your body, it is best to soak nuts, grains, and seeds in slightly acidic water for several hours before using them. To soak, cover with pure water and add 1–2 tablespoons of either fresh whey or lemon juice and soak overnight. Once soaked, you can dry them in a food dehydrator and keep them in an airtight container.

1. Mix chia seeds into yogurt. Do not add extra chia, as it can absorb up to 12 times its volume in liquid! One tablespoon of chia per parfait is plenty for an adult serving. If you are serving small children, you may wish to cut it down to as little as ¼ teaspoon per parfait and make smaller servings.

2. Place ¼ cup of yogurt in the bottom of 6 glasses.

3. Layer ingredients in each glass, adding 2 tablespoons walnuts, 1 tablespoon flaxseed, ½ sliced banana, and ¼ cup berries.

4. Add another ¼ cup of yogurt and repeat layers, topping the parfaits with the remaining ¼ cup yogurt per glass. Garnish with berries, and serve.

PER SERVING Calories: 649 | Fat: 38g | Protein: 12g | Sodium: 20mg | Fiber: 19g | Carbohydrates: 63g

Coconut Fruit and Nut Oatmeal

For a hot breakfast that is delicious, stays with you, and provides lasting satisfaction and energy until lunchtime, this power-packed oatmeal is a great way to start your day.

INGREDIENTS | SERVES 6

4 cups coconut water

1 peeled Jonathan or Granny Smith apple, cored and chopped

1 banana, peeled and sliced

½ cup raisins or dried cranberries (optional)

1 teaspoon sea salt

1 teaspoon cinnamon

2 cups oatmeal, soaked

½ cup oat bran, soaked

1. In a saucepan, mix coconut water, apple, banana, raisins, salt, and cinnamon; bring to a simmer.

2. Add oatmeal and oat bran; bring to a full rolling boil. Cook until oats are soft, about 3–5 minutes.

3. Remove from heat. Allow oats to cool to about 100°F. Serve with raw honey, chopped nuts, and coconut milk.

PER SERVING Calories: 183 | Fat: 3g | Protein: 6g | Sodium: 558mg | Fiber: 7g | Carbohydrates: 38g

Honey Coconut Quinoa

Quinoa is a great way to enjoy a delicious hot cereal that is gluten free!

1 cup quinoa

Filtered water to cover quinoa, plus 2 cups

1 tablespoon lemon juice

1 teaspoon sea salt

¼ cup ground flaxseed

1 tablespoon coconut oil

Raw honey, to taste

1 cup unsweetened desiccated coconut

1 teaspoon cinnamon

½ cup coconut milk

½ cup chopped almonds, soaked and dehydrated

Desiccated Coconut

Desiccated coconut is different from shredded coconut—it is more finely shredded and contains much less moisture than coconut that has just been shredded and dehydrated. As with shredded coconut, desiccated coconut is often sweetened, so watch the package labels when purchasing this product.

1. Place quinoa in a bowl and cover with water. Add lemon juice and allow quinoa to soak overnight.

2. Drain water and rinse quinoa in a fine mesh sieve.

3. Mix quinoa, 2 cups filtered water, and sea salt in a heavy-bottomed saucepan. Bring to a boil; reduce to a simmer. Cover with a lid; continue to cook for about 5–10 minutes, or until liquid is absorbed and quinoa can be fluffed with a fork.

4. Remove from heat; stir in flaxseed, coconut oil, honey, desiccated coconut, and cinnamon. Top with coconut milk and chopped almonds. Serve with berries or your favorite fruit.

PER SERVING Calories: 312 | Fat: 22g | Protein: 8g | Sodium: 396mg | Fiber: 7g | Carbohydrates: 25g

Coconut Pancake Syrup

This yummy coconut pancake syrup is a great way to add a little sweetness to your morning. If you are watching your sugar intake, even though this recipe uses natural coconut sugar, be careful not to overdo it!

INGREDIENTS | MAKES 1 CUP

1 (13.5-ounce) can coconut milk

1 cup coconut sugar

1 teaspoon potato starch flour

2 teaspoons filtered water

2 tablespoons desiccated coconut

1 teaspoon vanilla extract

Coconut Sugar

Most natural sugars can raise your blood sugar! Coconut sugar is a type of palm sugar and comes in many forms, from raw unrefined organic sugar to highly refined coconut sugar. Coconut sugar that has been processed and refined is not much different from white cane sugar. The less processed the sugar, the better an option for sweetening, but if you are diabetic, you may want to substitute liquid stevia or another low-glycemic sweetener.

1. Mix coconut milk and sugar in a saucepan until sugar is dissolved.

2. Bring to a boil; reduce heat to a simmer, stirring constantly, to prevent syrup from burning.

3. Mix potato starch with 2 teaspoons water; pour into syrup mixture, stirring constantly as you pour.

4. Bring to a boil; cook until slightly thickened, about 2 minutes.

5. Remove from heat; stir in desiccated coconut and vanilla. Serve with pancakes or waffles.

PER 1 TABLESPOON SERVING | Calories: 100 | Fat: 5g | Protein: 1g | Sodium: 3mg | Fiber: 0g | Carbohydrates: 14g

Coconut Pan-Fried Potatoes

Potatoes are a great source of potassium and vitamin C. They are also high in carbohydrates, so they need to be balanced with plenty of healthy fats. Cooking potatoes in coconut oil gives them a nice crispy outside, and also helps your body absorb the vitamins in the potatoes.

INGREDIENTS | SERVES 8

4 strips good-quality bacon

¼ cup unsweetened shredded coconut

6 medium red potatoes, cubed

1 medium onion, chopped

1 red bell pepper, diced (optional)

1 clove garlic

1–2 tablespoons coconut oil

Sea salt and black pepper, to taste

1. In a skillet, fry bacon and shredded coconut together until bacon is crispy. Cut bacon into ½" pieces.

2. Drain bacon grease; add potatoes, onion, bell pepper, garlic, and coconut oil.

3. Cook on medium heat until potatoes are tender and start to turn golden brown and slightly crispy on the edges.

4. Add salt and pepper, to taste.

PER SERVING Calories: 153 | Fat: 3g | Protein: 5g | Sodium: 104mg | Fiber: 3g | Carbohydrates: 27g

Banana and Coconut Breakfast Muffins

These banana muffins made with coconut flour are a great low-carb alternative.

INGREDIENTS | MAKES 1 DOZEN MUFFINS

½ cup coconut flour

¼ teaspoon sea salt

½ teaspoon baking powder

4 eggs

¼ cup coconut oil

¼ cup honey

2–3 ripe bananas, mashed

½ cup nuts, soaked and dehydrated

1. Preheat the oven to 350°F.

2. Mix all ingredients; scoop into a greased muffin pan.

3. Bake for 15 minutes, or until golden brown. Serve warm.

PER 1 MUFFIN | Calories: 151 | Fat: 9g | Protein: 4g | Sodium: 92mg | Fiber: 3g | Carbohydrates: 15g

Coconut Flour

Coconut flour is dehydrated coconut meat that has had most of the oil removed and been ground to a powdery consistency. It is not good for thickening sauces, but it works very well for baking. It is high in protein and gluten free.

Creamy Coconut-Mango Quinoa

This yummy coconut-mango quinoa cereal is so much like a dessert that it is hard to believe you are eating something so packed with nutrients!

INGREDIENTS | SERVES 6

3 cups coconut milk

1 cup water

2 teaspoons cinnamon

2 cups quinoa, soaked and rinsed

1 mango, peeled and cubed

1 tablespoon raw honey

---

1. In a heavy-bottomed medium saucepan, mix coconut milk, water, cinnamon, and quinoa. Cover and cook on medium-low heat for about 30 minutes, or until quinoa can be fluffed with a fork.

2. Remove from heat; add mango and raw honey. Serve hot.

PER SERVING Calories: 466 | Fat: 28g | Protein: 11g | Sodium: 18mg | Fiber: 5g | Carbohydrates: 49g

Quinoa

Quinoa is a grain-like seed that can be used much like rice, and can be ground to make flour. Quinoa is a traditional staple of South America, where the Incas domesticated it from a wild form that grew in the native Andes mountains. Quinoa was replaced by wheat after the Spanish conquest, but has recently been rediscovered due to its high nutritional value.

Coconut Rice with Mangoes

Rice is not just a side dish! Try this fantastic hot rice cereal for a morning energy boost.

INGREDIENTS | SERVES 6

2 cups uncooked brown rice

6 cups filtered water, divided use

2 tablespoons whey or lemon juice

1 (13.5-ounce) can unsweetened coconut milk

¾ cup coconut sugar

1 teaspoon sea salt

2 ripe mangoes

3 cups fresh strawberries

1. Place rice in a bowl. Cover with 2 cups filtered water; add whey or lemon juice. Soak overnight.

2. Drain water and rinse rice in a colander. Add rice to a rice cooker with 4 cups filtered water; cook according to directions.

3. In a saucepan over medium heat, combine coconut milk, sugar, and salt. Stir until dissolved, about 3 minutes; bring to a boil.

4. Remove from heat; set aside ⅓ cup of coconut milk mixture.

5. Pour remaining coconut milk mixture over rice. Cover and allow to sit for 10–15 minutes.

6. Slice mangoes and strawberries. Serve rice topped with sliced fruit and coconut sauce.

PER SERVING Calories: 518 | Fat: 16g | Protein: 7g | Sodium: 405mg | Fiber: 5g | Carbohydrates: 92g

Country Fried Steak Strips

If you need more protein in the morning, try these hearty country fried steaks with mushroom coconut sauce.

INGREDIENTS | SERVES 6

1 egg, well beaten

1 recipe finely crushed Garlic Herb Coconut Crackers (see Chapter 12)

½ cup coconut flour

1½ teaspoons sea salt, divided use

½ teaspoon pepper, plus more to taste

½ teaspoon garlic powder

⅛ teaspoon dried basil

6 (3-ounce) beef cubed steaks

3 tablespoons coconut oil

½ pound small portobello mushrooms, chopped

1 small onion, finely chopped

1 clove garlic

1 tablespoon potato starch flour

1 cup coconut milk

1. Place egg and crushed crackers in separate shallow bowls.

2. In another shallow bowl, mix coconut flour, ½ teaspoon salt, ½ teaspoon pepper, garlic powder, and dried basil.

3. Dredge cube steaks in flour mixture. Dip in egg, then in crumbs.

4. In a large skillet, melt 1 tablespoon coconut oil and cook steaks for 3–5 minutes on each side, or until no longer pink in the center. Remove steaks from skillet.

5. Sauté mushrooms and onion with 2 tablespoons coconut oil, scraping the meat drippings from the bottom of the pan.

6. Add garlic, 1 teaspoon salt, and pepper to taste. Sprinkle with potato starch flour and add coconut milk, whisking in a little at a time, until you have a thick mushroom sauce.

7. If the sauce is thinner than you like, mix a small amount of potato starch flour with a little water, and stir it into the sauce. If the sauce is too thick, add a little more coconut milk until you reach the desired consistency. Serve cube steaks with mushroom gravy.

PER SERVING Calories: 258 | Fat: 19g | Protein: 7g | Sodium: 701mg | Fiber: 8g | Carbohydrates: 18g

Breakfast Casserole

This delicious hot breakfast casserole can be made the night before and then popped in the oven in the morning for a nice alternative to cereal.

INGREDIENTS | SERVES 6

6 fresh pastured eggs
3 tablespoons coconut ghee, melted
1 cup coconut milk
8 ounces cream cheese, softened
½ teaspoon sea salt
¼ teaspoon fresh black pepper
4 strips thick-cut bacon, cooked and crumbled
¼ cup green onions, minced
½ red bell pepper, diced
1 clove garlic, pressed
¼ cup coconut flour
1 cup aged raw Cheddar cheese, shredded

1. Preheat the oven to 350°F.

2. Beat eggs, 2 tablespoons of ghee, coconut milk, cream cheese, salt, and pepper in a bowl.

3. Save out 1 tablespoon each of bacon and green onion; set aside.

4. Mix remaining bacon and green onion into the egg mixture.

5. Add bell pepper and garlic; whisk in coconut flour.

6. Melt remaining tablespoon of ghee into the bottom of a 7" × 11" baking dish. Pour in egg mixture and sprinkle top with Cheddar cheese and reserved bacon and onions.

7. Bake, uncovered, for 25–30 minutes, or until a toothpick inserted in the center comes out clean.

PER SERVING Calories: 460 | Fat: 41g | Protein: 17g | Sodium: 632mg | Fiber: 2g | Carbohydrates: 8g

Crispy Coconut Hash Brown Potatoes

These crispy coconut hash brown potatoes are a perfect companion to the Coconut Scramble or Breakfast Casserole (see recipes in this chapter).

INGREDIENTS | SERVES 6

6 medium russet potatoes
1 medium onion
½ cup grated fresh young coconut meat
1–2 cloves garlic
2 tablespoons coconut ghee
Sea salt and pepper, to taste

1. Scrub and shred potatoes. Peel and shred onion.

2. Mix potato, onion, and coconut meat in a bowl. Using a garlic press, press garlic into the bowl with the potatoes and onion.

3. Melt 1 tablespoon ghee in the bottom of a hot skillet. Add handfuls of the potato mixture; cook, covered, until crispy on one side, about 2–3 minutes.

4. Remove lid; dab 1 tablespoon ghee onto uncooked sides. Turn hash browns over; cook another 2–3 minutes, or until done. Add salt and pepper, to taste.

PER SERVING Calories: 217 | Fat: 7g | Protein: 4g | Sodium: 15mg | Fiber: 6g | Carbohydrates: 39g

Fishing Boat Breakfast

Enjoy this fresh tuna breakfast adapted from a traditional New Zealand fisherman's breakfast.

INGREDIENTS | SERVES 6

2–3 tablespoons coconut ghee
3 pounds fresh wild-caught tuna steaks
Flesh of 1 young fresh coconut, grated
Juice of 2 limes

Omega-3s

Omega-3 fatty acids are essential for weight loss, memory, and your overall health. This tasty traditional fisherman's breakfast combines the omega-3s from fish with the medium-chain fatty acids of coconut oil. It's a great way to improve your memory, energy, and to strengthen your immune system.

1. Melt 1 tablespoon of ghee in a hot skillet. Add tuna; cook, covered, for about 10 minutes, then turn and cook until tuna can be flaked with a fork, about 5 minutes.

2. Flake tuna into chunks with a fork; add shredded coconut and additional ghee as needed. Cook for another 5 minutes, stirring occasionally.

3. Squeeze lime juice over tuna. Serve with Fluffy Coconut Pancakes and Waffles (see recipe in this chapter) or warm Coconut Flour Tortillas/Crepes (see recipe in Chapter 17).

PER SERVING Calories: 597 | Fat: 38g | Protein: 54g | Sodium: 101mg | Fiber: 6g | Carbohydrates: 11g

Cream of Buckwheat Cereal

Hot cereal is a great way to start the day, especially on those cold winter or early spring mornings!

INGREDIENTS | SERVES 6

2 cups whole buckwheat groats

3 cups coconut milk

3 cups filtered water

½ teaspoon sea salt

2 tablespoons coconut oil

Buckwheat

Buckwheat, like quinoa, is a seed and is not related to wheat at all. It can be made into flour and is gluten free, and works well as an alternative to wheat in making baked goods and noodles.

1. With a coffee grinder, grind groats until they are the consistency of uncooked cream of wheat cereal (not fine like flour, but coarse and grainy).

2. In a medium saucepan, mix coconut milk and water. Bring to a simmer; stir in buckwheat. Continue to simmer until cereal is thickened and comes to a boil, about 5 minutes.

3. Remove from heat; add salt and coconut oil. Serve with raw honey, maple syrup, or berries.

PER SERVING Calories: 456 | Fat: 31g | Protein: 10g | Sodium: 209mg | Fiber: 6g | Carbohydrates: 44g

Coconut Scramble

Eggs are a great way to start the day! Known by many as nature's perfect food, eggs have a natural balance of protein and fats for a filling and satisfying morning meal. Try this coconut milk version of one of America's favorite breakfasts: scrambled eggs.

INGREDIENTS | SERVES 6

10 large fresh pastured eggs

½ cup coconut milk

1 small onion, minced

1 small clove garlic, pressed

Sea salt and freshly ground black pepper, to taste

2 tablespoons coconut ghee

½ cup raw Cheddar cheese, grated (optional)

1. In a bowl, beat together eggs, coconut milk, onion, garlic, salt, and pepper.

2. Melt ghee in the bottom of a heavy-bottomed skillet.

3. Cook, stirring occasionally, for about 5 minutes, until eggs are done.

4. Sprinkle with cheese; cover for 1–2 minutes, or until cheese is melted. Serve hot.

PER SERVING Calories: 200 | Fat: 17g | Protein: 11g | Sodium: 120mg | Fiber: 0g | Carbohydrates: 2g

CHAPTER 12

Appetizers

Coconut Fruit Kebabs

This is a fun way to bring new life to fruit! Kebabs can be made up ahead of time and kept in the refrigerator until time to serve.

INGREDIENTS | SERVES 6

1 large red apple, cut into 12 bite-sized cubes

1 teaspoon lemon juice

1 mango, cut into 12 bite-sized cubes

12 seedless grapes

12 pineapple chunks

12 fresh strawberries, capped

6 wooden skewers

1. Place apple chunks in a resealable sandwich bag.

2. Add lemon juice; shake bag to coat apple pieces evenly.

3. Put apples, mangoes, grapes, pineapple, and strawberries on skewers in an alternating pattern until all fruit is used up, about 10 pieces of fruit on each skewer. Serve with Coconut Fruit Dip (see recipe in this chapter).

PER SERVING Calories: 70 | Fat: 0g | Protein: 1g | Sodium: 2mg | Fiber: 2g | Carbohydrates: 18g

Coconut Curry Chicken Balls

Impress guests or surprise your family with this tasty treat! These can be served alone or as an individual serving-sized cheese ball to be spread on Garlic Herb Coconut Crackers (see recipe in this chapter) or toasted bread.

INGREDIENTS | SERVES 6

½ cup grated unsweetened coconut meat

1 tablespoon Coconut Cream Mayonnaise (see Chapter 20)

4 tablespoons cream cheese, softened

½ cup cooked chicken, chopped

¼ cup pecans, chopped

1 tablespoon onion, minced

1 clove garlic, minced

½ teaspoon curry powder

¼ teaspoon sea salt

1. Preheat the oven to 350°F.

2. Spread grated coconut evenly on a baking sheet and toast until lightly browned, about 10 minutes.

3. In a small mixing bowl, blend together Coconut Mayonnaise and cream cheese until smooth.

4. Add chicken, pecans, onion, garlic, curry, and salt; mix well.

5. Form chicken mixture into 1" balls.

6. Roll balls in toasted coconut until well coated.

7. Place chicken balls on a baking sheet and cover with plastic wrap. Chill for 1 hour before serving.

PER SERVING Calories: 170 | Fat: 16g | Protein: 5g | Sodium: 168mg | Fiber: 2g | Carbohydrates: 3g

Caribbean Crab Dip

If you are looking for something a little different, this is an easy-to-prepare vacation from the standard corn chips and salsa. Tantalize your guests with this simple-to-make, tasty, and somewhat exotic appetizer.

INGREDIENTS | SERVES 6

¼ cup cilantro
1 cup unsweetened coconut milk
1 tablespoon hot sauce
Juice of 2 freshly squeezed limes
½ teaspoon sea salt
Freshly ground black pepper, to taste
1 pound crab meat
1 (5-ounce) bag plantain chips

Plantain Chips

Plantain bananas are not as soft and sweet as the bananas that you typically find in your grocery store. Most grocery stores also sell plantain, which can be thinly sliced and deep fried in coconut oil to make chips for dipping. You can buy plantain chips at a Latin market if you have one in your area, but if you want to avoid trans fats, you will want to get chips that have been fried either in lard or in coconut oil because most other fats cannot withstand the heat needed to deep-fry foods.

1. Separate out about 6 sprigs of cilantro to use as a garnish; finely chop the remaining cilantro.

2. Mix coconut milk, cilantro, hot sauce, and lime juice in a bowl.

3. Season with salt and pepper.

4. Stir in crabmeat and let stand for 10–15 minutes.

5. Use a slotted spoon to scoop crabmeat into 6 individual serving bowls. Add remaining sprigs of cilantro as a garnish, and serve with plantain chips.

PER SERVING Calories: 232 | Fat: 11g | Protein: 17g | Sodium: 443mg | Fiber: 1g | Carbohydrates: 15g

Coconut-Tuna Lettuce Cups

The omega-3s, combined with the delicious flavor of sautéed tuna and the fat-burning power of coconut oil, will make this tasty appetizer a real hit!

INGREDIENTS | SERVES 6

1½ cups coconut milk
1 tablespoon chili sauce
½ teaspoon fish sauce
1 tablespoon virgin coconut oil
1½ pounds fresh tuna, cubed
Zest and juice of 1 lime
¼ teaspoon sea salt
1 clove garlic, minced
1 mango, diced
1¼ cups cilantro, finely chopped
2 avocados, diced
2 green onions, finely chopped
6 leaves romaine lettuce

1. In a saucepan, bring coconut milk, chili sauce, and fish sauce to a simmer on medium heat. Stir until about half of the liquid has evaporated, about 5 minutes. Remove from heat.

2. Melt coconut oil in a skillet; add tuna. Add lime zest, salt, and garlic; sauté over medium heat until tuna is cooked through, about 3–5 minutes.

3. Set aside ¼ cup of the diced mango and a few sprigs of cilantro to use as a garnish.

4. Add avocado and remaining mango to tuna; pour coconut sauce over tuna mixture. Toss lightly until well coated.

5. Add remaining cilantro and green onions; squeeze lime juice over top. Serve on romaine leaves, garnished with mango and cilantro.

PER SERVING Calories: 432 | Fat: 30g | Protein: 29g | Sodium: 197mg | Fiber: 6g | Carbohydrates: 15g

Coconut-Cashew Shrimp Balls

This tasty cheese ball is sure to be a real party pleaser. For a little more zing, you can add 1 jalapeño pepper to your food processor with the other ingredients. Remove seeds for medium heat, but leave them in if you like it hot!

INGREDIENTS | **SERVES 6**

½ cup unsweetened shredded coconut

½ cup cashew pieces, finely chopped

2 (8-ounce) packages cream cheese

1½ cups cooked shrimp, peeled and deveined

¼ cup mango salsa

2 green onions, finely chopped

Shredded Coconut

Most of the shredded coconut that you find in the store is sweetened. To avoid the added sugar, use unsweetened shredded coconut, or make your own by using a fine grater and shredding the coconut meat. Once you have shredded it, you can dehydrate the coconut in a food dehydrator or by putting it in the oven on the lowest temperature possible. If you want your coconut to remain raw, you will need to keep the temperature at or below 110°F.

1. Preheat the oven to 350°F.

2. Place coconut and cashews on a baking sheet; bake until golden brown, about 3–5 minutes. Do not overcook!

3. In a food processor, place cream cheese, shrimp, salsa, and onions; mix until well blended.

4. Place cream cheese mixture in the refrigerator and chill for 1 hour.

5. Shape into 1" balls; roll in toasted coconut-cashew mixture. Serve with plantain chips or Garlic Herb Coconut Crackers (see recipe in this chapter).

PER SERVING Calories: 412 | Fat: 35g | Protein: 16g | Sodium: 349mg | Fiber: 2g | Carbohydrates: 10g

Three-Layer Coconut-Shrimp-Cheese Spread

*This layered dip is a wonderful change from your standard seven-layer
bean dip, and is sure to be a hit with family and friends!*

INGREDIENTS | SERVES 8

1 cup shredded coconut
2 (8-ounce) packages cream cheese
½ cup pineapple tidbits, drained
2 tablespoons hot sauce
1 (4.5-ounce) can salad shrimp, drained
¼ cup coconut cream
1 cup mango salsa

1. Preheat the oven to 350°F.

2. Spread coconut over bottom of a baking sheet; bake until golden brown, about 3–5 minutes.

3. In a food processor, mix cream cheese, pineapple, hot sauce, shrimp, and coconut cream until smooth. Make sure pineapple and shrimp are well drained.

4. Spread cream cheese mixture in the bottom of a 9" × 9" baking dish.

5. Spread mango salsa over cream cheese layer.

6. Top with toasted coconut; chill for 1 hour before serving. Serve with Garlic Herb Coconut Crackers (see recipe in this chapter), plantain chips, or tortilla chips.

PER SERVING Calories: 320 | Fat: 27g | Protein: 7g | Sodium: 310mg | Fiber: 2g | Carbohydrates: 15g

Fried Coconut Eggplant

Make sure that your oil is hot enough before frying. This prevents the oil from being absorbed by the eggplant, and you'll get a crisper crust on the outside.

INGREDIENTS | SERVES 6

3 eggs
2 tablespoons coconut milk
½ cup coconut flour
1 teaspoon sea salt
½ teaspoon black pepper
½ teaspoon garlic powder
3 medium eggplants
Coconut oil, as needed

How do I know if the oil is hot enough for frying?

A quick trick to test the temperature of your oil is to place the end of your wooden spoon handle in the hot oil. If you see bubbles moving from the end of the wooden spoon, it is hot enough. If you don't see bubbles, it is not.

1. In a wide dish, beat eggs and coconut milk together until well blended.

2. In a separate wide dish, mix coconut flour, salt, pepper, and garlic powder.

3. Slice eggplant into ¼" slices; dip in egg mixture, then dredge in coconut flour mixture.

4. Heat enough coconut oil to cover the bottom of a heavy-bottomed frying skillet.

5. When oil is hot enough for frying, place eggplant in oil and sauté until golden brown, about 3 minutes. Turn and repeat on second side. Place on paper towel to drain. Serve with Spicy Coconut Dipping Sauce (see recipe in this chapter).

PER SERVING Calories: 309 | Fat: 23g | Protein: 7g | Sodium: 429mg | Fiber: 13g | Carbohydrates: 23g

Coconut-Ginger Mussels with Bacon

This appetizer makes a beautiful presentation and is a great way to start your meal. This goes well with several Thai dishes that can be found in Chapters 13 and 14.

INGREDIENTS | SERVES 6

10 slices thick-cut bacon

2 cups young coconut water

3 teaspoons fresh ginger, grated

1 tablespoon soy sauce

3 pounds small mussels

Selecting Mussels

When shopping for mussels, never choose mussels that are cracked, chipped, or broken. The mussels should be closed, never open. Mussels should be soaked in fresh clean water for about 20 minutes before cooking. Once the mussels have been soaked, scrub them with a vegetable brush to remove the beard and any dirt or other impurities.

1. Cut bacon strips in half lengthwise then cut into ½" pieces. Fry bacon, covered, in a heavy-bottomed skillet until nearly crisp. Pour off grease.

2. Add coconut water, ginger, and soy sauce; simmer on medium low for 2 minutes, then increase to medium-high heat.

3. Add mussels; cook, covered, shaking skillet occasionally, until mussels open, about 5–10 minutes. Discard any mussels that do not open.

4. Serve mussels in shallow bowls; pour coconut bacon broth over top.

PER SERVING Calories: 164 | Fat: 9g | Protein: 14g | Sodium: 865mg | Fiber: 1g | Carbohydrates: 5g

Coconut Shrimp with Pineapple-Cilantro Dip

This recipe takes the classic coconut shrimp recipe and incorporates coconut meat, flour, milk, and oil to give you the benefits of the whole coconut!

INGREDIENTS | SERVES 6

½ coconut, shredded
1 cup bread crumbs
Sea salt and black pepper, to taste
⅓ cup coconut flour
2 eggs
4 tablespoons coconut milk
12 large shrimp, peeled and deveined
Coconut oil, as needed
1 cup fresh pineapple, cubed
2 cloves garlic
¼ cup cilantro, chopped
1 jalapeño pepper, seeded

Buying Shrimp

When buying shrimp or other seafood, you can make sure they are fresh by smelling the package. If you can smell a strong fishy smell through the packaging, they are not fresh. If you buy fresh shrimp, it should be used within 24 hours. If you do not live in an area where you can buy fresh shrimp, it is better to get it frozen.

1. Preheat the oven to 400°F.

2. In food processor, combine shredded coconut, bread crumbs, salt, and pepper. Place in a shallow bowl.

3. Place coconut flour in another shallow bowl.

4. In a third shallow bowl, beat eggs and coconut milk together until well mixed.

5. Coat each shrimp in flour, dip in egg, and then dredge in coconut mixture.

6. Melt enough coconut oil to cover the bottom of a heavy-bottomed skillet about ½" deep. When oil is hot enough for frying, add shrimp and sauté until golden brown, turning when needed, about 1 minute on each side. When cooked through, remove shrimp and place on a paper towel to drain.

7. In food processor, pulse pineapple, garlic, cilantro, and jalapeño until coarsely chopped. Serve with shrimp.

PER SERVING Calories: 210 | Fat: 13g | Protein: 6g | Sodium: 134mg | Fiber: 3g | Carbohydrates: 18g

Garlic Herb Coconut Crackers

These crispy crackers make a great companion to the Coconut-Cashew Shrimp Balls or the Coconut Curry Chicken Balls that can be found in this chapter.

INGREDIENTS | SERVES 6

½ cup coconut flour

¼ teaspoon sea salt

¼ teaspoon garlic powder

⅛ teaspoon rosemary

⅛ teaspoon dried basil

1 tablespoon sesame seeds

1 tablespoon flaxseeds

2½ teaspoons active dry yeast

1 teaspoon virgin coconut oil

3 tablespoons filtered water

Using Seeds in Your Recipes

For a nice crunch, soak your seeds overnight and then dry them in a food dehydrator before adding them to your recipes. Not only does this give your seeds a nice crunchy texture, it makes the nutrients in the seeds more bioavailable.

1. Preheat the oven to 350°F.

2. Mix all ingredients in food processor except water; pulse until well mixed.

3. Add water a little at a time until dough forms. Remove from food processor; form into a ball.

4. Use a small amount of flour to dust your work surface; use a rolling pin to roll out the dough to ¼" thick.

5. Use a sharp knife or pastry cutter to cut the dough into 1" squares.

6. Poke 4 holes in each square to prevent the dough from bubbling or curling on the edges. Arrange squares on a baking sheet; bake for 15 minutes, or until golden brown around the edges.

7. Remove from oven and allow to cool. Store in an airtight container.

PER SERVING Calories: 51 | Fat: 2g | Protein: 3g | Sodium: 100mg | Fiber: 4g | Carbohydrates: 6g

Coconut Fruit Dip

This yummy fruit dip balances the sweetness of the fruit with healthy protein and fats. If you combine natural sugars with protein and good fats, it helps prevent insulin spikes, which evens out your blood sugar and prevents your body from storing all of those sugars as fat.

INGREDIENTS | SERVES 6

8 ounces cream cheese, softened

1 (15-ounce) can cream of coconut

1 cup heavy whipping cream

Dairy

For the best results, for flavor and for health, use fresh unprocessed dairy products whenever possible. If you do not have access to fresh dairy, look for cream and milk that are unhomogenized. Always avoid ultrapasteurized dairy products. Check labels to make sure cream is only cream without additives, and cheeses should only contain cultured milk, rennet, and salt.

1. Place cream cheese in a mixing bowl; add coconut cream. Beat together until smooth.

2. Continue beating; add whipping cream and beat until stiff peaks form. Serve with Coconut Fruit Kebabs (see recipe in this chapter).

PER SERVING Calories: 514 | Fat: 39g | Protein: 4g | Sodium: 160mg | Fiber: 0g | Carbohydrates: 40g

Coconut-Garlic Chicken Bites

The unique flavor of cumin complements the avocado without being overbearing. This dip is perfect with a south-of-the-border menu or spread on warm tortilla chips.

INGREDIENTS | **SERVES 6**

1 egg, lightly beaten
2 tablespoons coconut milk
½ cup coconut flour
1 cup unsweetened shredded coconut
½ teaspoon sea salt
¼ teaspoon black pepper
¼ teaspoon garlic powder
1 pound chicken breast, cubed
½ cup coconut ghee, melted

Coconut Ghee

Coconut ghee is made by melting 2 parts butter, straining out the milk solids with a piece of cheesecloth, and then adding 1 part coconut oil. Coconut ghee can last for several months and has fantastic flavor.

1. Preheat the oven to 400°F.

2. In a wide shallow bowl, beat egg and coconut milk together.

3. In a second wide shallow bowl, mix coconut flour, coconut, sea salt, pepper, and garlic powder.

4. Dip chicken into egg mixture, then in coconut mixture. Place on baking sheet and drizzle with ghee.

5. Bake 20 minutes, or until chicken bites are browned and cooked through. Serve with Spicy Coconut Dipping Sauce (see recipe in this chapter).

PER SERVING Calories: 347 | Fat: 26g | Protein: 20g | Sodium: 259mg | Fiber: 6g | Carbohydrates: 10g

Crispy Coconut Potato Skins

For all the benefits of flavor combined with healthy whole foods, this classic appetizer is even better when cooked in coconut oil.

INGREDIENTS | SERVES 6

6 medium russet potatoes
6 strips thick-cut bacon
Coconut oil, as needed
Coarsely ground sea salt
Freshly ground black pepper
½ cup Cheddar cheese, grated
½ cup sour cream
2 green onions, chopped

1. Preheat the oven to 375°F.

2. Scrub potatoes and pierce with a fork; bake for 30 minutes, until done. Remove from oven.

3. Place bacon on a baking sheet; place them in the oven. Cook for 15–20 minutes, or until crisp. Remove from oven and drain on a paper towel, then crumble.

4. Cut potatoes in half lengthwise and scoop out flesh with a spoon, leaving about ¼" of potato on the skin.

5. Increase oven temperature to 400°F.

6. Rub potato skins inside and out with coconut oil. Sprinkle with salt and place skin-side down on roasting rack.

7. Bake for 10 minutes, then flip over and bake another 10 minutes.

8. Remove from oven and turn skin-side down. Sprinkle with pepper, cheese, and bacon.

9. Return to the oven and broil until cheese begins to bubble, about 5 minutes. Remove from the oven, and serve with sour cream and green onions.

PER SERVING Calories: 308 | Fat: 20g | Protein: 9g | Sodium: 334mg | Fiber: 4g | Carbohydrates: 26g

Coconut Spinach-Artichoke Dip and Pita Chips

This spinach-artichoke dip will have you coming back for more, but without the guilt when you make it with your own homemade coconut mayonnaise.

INGREDIENTS | SERVES 8

4 large artichokes, steamed
1 pound fresh baby spinach
2 jalapeños, seeded and chopped
1 cup shredded Parmesan cheese
1 cup Coconut Cream Mayonnaise (see Chapter 20)
4 ounces cream cheese
1 cup shredded mild white Cheddar
Sea salt, to taste
1 package whole-wheat pita bread
Coconut oil, as needed

Hot Peppers

When using hot peppers in recipes, you can control the heat of the dish by removing the seeds for a milder heat or leaving them in for more kick if you like it hot!

1. Preheat the oven to 400°F.

2. Remove outer leaves from artichokes; roughly chop hearts.

3. In a food processor, mix artichoke hearts and all other ingredients except pita bread and oil; pulse until coarsely chopped and evenly mixed.

4. Place mixture in a 9" × 9" baking dish and bake until golden brown, about 8–10 minutes.

5. To make pita chips: Preheat the oven to 350°F. Cut the pita bread into triangles. Use a basting brush to coat the bread with a thin layer of coconut oil and sprinkle with sea salt. Place evenly on a baking sheet; bake for 20 minutes, or until crunchy. Remove from oven and cool before serving with dip.

PER SERVING Calories: 517 | Fat: 37g | Protein: 18g | Sodium: 659mg | Fiber: 7g | Carbohydrates: 34g

Sweet Potato Fries

Sweet potato fries are a flavorful change from your typical French fried potatoes. You can season them with savory herbs and spices or sprinkle them with sweetened cinnamon mixed into coconut ghee to satisfy your need for a sweet treat!

INGREDIENTS | SERVES 6

3–4 medium-sized sweet potatoes
4 tablespoons coconut oil
Sea salt, to taste

1. Preheat the oven to 400°F.

2. Clean sweet potatoes thoroughly and cut lengthwise into ½" slices. Cut slices into long strips.

3. Use a basting brush to coat potato strips with coconut oil; place on a baking sheet. Salt lightly.

4. Bake for 25 minutes, or until edges are lightly browned and potatoes are cooked through.

PER SERVING Calories: 75 | Fat: 2g | Protein: 1g | Sodium: 36mg | Fiber: 2g | Carbohydrates: 13g

Spicy Coconut Dipping Sauce

This spicy dipping sauce is a great companion to the Fried Coconut Eggplant or the Coconut-Garlic Chicken Bites in this chapter.

INGREDIENTS | YIELDS 1 CUP

1 cup unsweetened coconut milk

1 tablespoon cornstarch

4 teaspoons fresh ginger, grated

1 or 2 red poblano chilies, seeded

2 cloves garlic

2 teaspoons freshly squeezed lime juice

1. Mix coconut milk and cornstarch together in a small heavy-bottomed saucepan over medium heat. Bring to a boil, stirring constantly for 1 minute, and allow sauce to thicken.

2. In a food processor, mix ginger, chilies, garlic, and lime juice. Add to coconut milk mixture and remove from heat. Chill before serving.

PER 1 TABLESPOON | Calories: 33 | Fat: 3g | Protein: 0g | Sodium: 3mg | Fiber: 0g | Carbohydrates: 2g

Meats and Poultry

Coconut Chicken Alfredo

This creamy Coconut Chicken Alfredo is a great way to use coconut milk! For a dairy-free version, just leave out the Parmesan cheese and use coconut oil instead of coconut ghee.

INGREDIENTS | SERVES 6

3 boneless, skinless chicken breasts

1 cup broccoli florets

3 cloves fresh garlic, minced

1 teaspoon black pepper

2 teaspoons rosemary

4 tablespoons coconut ghee

2 (13.5-ounce) cans coconut milk

2 teaspoons potato starch flour

½ cup grated Parmesan cheese

2 teaspoons sea salt

2 teaspoons onion powder

1 (16-ounce) package uncooked whole-grain linguine

Gluten-Free Pastas

Pasta is usually made from highly refined flour and filled with simple carbohydrates, which can cause blood sugar spikes. If you eat pasta, buy whole-wheat or gluten-free pastas. These are very good, but they are very dense in comparison and have a heavier texture. You may like to try quinoa or buckwheat pastas, or a pasta made of a blend of whole-grain flours.

1. Cut chicken and broccoli into bite-sized pieces; set aside.

2. In a large sauté pan, sauté garlic, pepper, and rosemary in 2 tablespoons of ghee for about 1 minute. Add chicken and cook another 5 minutes, or until cooked through.

3. Add broccoli florets and cover. Cook for another 2 minutes, or until broccoli is tender but not soft. Remove chicken and broccoli from the pan; cover and set aside.

4. In a separate bowl, mix coconut milk and potato starch flour until well mixed. Add remaining ghee to the sauté pan with the coconut milk mixture and cook on medium-low heat, stirring constantly and scraping the bottom to loosen chicken drippings, until mixture comes to a simmer.

5. Whisk in Parmesan cheese, salt, and onion powder. Continue to cook until sauce is thick enough to coat the spoon, about 2–3 minutes.

6. Prepare pasta according to directions on the package. Drain and serve with chicken and broccoli, then top with coconut Alfredo sauce and sprinkle with additional Parmesan cheese, if desired.

PER SERVING Calories: 702 | Fat: 40g | Protein: 31g | Sodium: 969mg | Fiber: 1g | Carbohydrates: 63g

Chicken with Garlic-Coconut Sauce

This Colombian-style chicken dish is delicious with Coconut Rice (see Chapter 15).

INGREDIENTS | SERVES 6

4 tablespoons coconut oil, melted
1 tablespoon coconut vinegar
3 boneless, skinless chicken breasts
1 teaspoon garlic powder
½ teaspoon cumin plus 1 dash
Freshly ground black pepper, to taste
1 small white onion, finely chopped
1 red bell pepper, diced
2 cloves garlic, minced
¼ teaspoon sea salt
1 dash oregano powder
1 dash saffron powder
1 teaspoon potato starch flour
1 (13.5-ounce) can coconut milk

1. Combine coconut oil and vinegar in a resealsable plastic bag; shake until evenly mixed.

2. Slice the chicken breasts into ½" strips; place inside the plastic bag with the oil and vinegar mixture and gently toss to coat.

3. In a small bowl, mix together garlic powder, ½ teaspoon cumin, and black pepper. Sprinkle over chicken and allow chicken to marinate for at least 1 hour.

4. Heat a large heavy-bottomed skillet over medium-high heat. Empty contents of the resealable plastic bag into the skillet; sauté chicken strips for 3–5 minutes, or until golden brown. Remove chicken to a plate and set aside.

5. Add onion, red pepper, and garlic to the skillet. Season with salt, pepper, oregano, cumin, and saffron. Sauté vegetables until tender, about 3 minutes.

6. In another small bowl, whisk potato starch flour into coconut milk; add to the skillet with the chicken strips, red peppers, and onion. Cover and simmer for another 10 minutes. Serve over rice.

PER SERVING Calories: 283 | Fat: 23g | Protein: 15g | Sodium: 145mg | Fiber: 1g | Carbohydrates: 5g

Chicken Vindaloo

Chicken Vindaloo, with its exotic mixture of spices, is a popular dish in many parts of India. Indian recipes commonly use a variety of spices that most Americans would not expect to find in a savory dish.

INGREDIENTS | SERVES 6

1 pound boneless, skinless chicken thighs

2 tablespoons fresh ginger, minced

¼ cup coconut or palm vinegar

2 teaspoons ground coriander

2 teaspoons ground cumin

1 teaspoon ground cardamom

2 teaspoons chili paste with garlic

¼ teaspoon ground cinnamon

⅛ teaspoon ground cloves

6 cloves garlic, minced

1 tablespoon coconut oil

1 large white onion, diced

1 red bell pepper, diced

1 yellow bell pepper, diced

½ cup chicken broth

1 teaspoon sea salt

1 teaspoon potato starch flour

1 tablespoon water

¼ cup fresh cilantro, minced

4 cups cooked brown rice

1. Cut chicken into 1" cubes; combine with ginger, vinegar, coriander, cumin, cardamom, chili paste, cinnamon, cloves, and minced garlic in a resealable plastic bag. Marinate overnight in the refrigerator.

2. Heat coconut oil in a large skillet over medium-high heat. Add onion and sauté until onion is translucent, about 5 minutes.

3. Add chicken mixture and bell peppers; sauté another 5 minutes, or until chicken is browned. Add chicken broth and salt. Simmer, uncovered, for another 10–15 minutes.

4. In a small bowl, combine potato starch flour and water; add to skillet. Stir well and cook for another 1–2 minutes, or until sauce thickens. Stir in cilantro, and serve over rice.

PER SERVING Calories: 292 | Fat: 7g | Protein: 19g | Sodium: 493g | Fiber: 4g | Carbohydrates: 36g

Roasted Coconut Chicken

This delicious roasted whole chicken, with its combination of curry and coconut oil, is a real antioxidant blast! Your immune system will thank you.

INGREDIENTS | SERVES 6

2 tablespoons curry paste

2 tablespoons coconut oil

1 teaspoon fresh ginger, grated

1 teaspoon lemongrass, finely chopped

1 (13.5-ounce) can coconut milk

1 large roaster chicken

Curry

There are many varieties of curry pastes and powders. Curry is a combination of herbs and spices, and usually contains turmeric, coriander, and cumin along with a variety of other spices, and ranges from fiery to mild. Curry paste and curry are not interchangeable in recipes, since each curry powder and paste contains different ingredients. Curry pastes are wet seasonings, while curry powders are dry. There are many recipes for curry pastes and powders available and many commercially prepared curries that you can purchase.

1. Preheat the oven to 375°F.

2. Combine curry paste, coconut oil, ginger, and lemongrass with 2 tablespoons coconut milk; brush it over the chicken with a basting brush.

3. Place the chicken in a roasting pan and pour remaining coconut milk over the chicken. Roast for about 1½ hours, basting occasionally with coconut milk.

4. Remove chicken from the oven and leave to stand for 10 minutes before carving.

PER SERVING Calories: 368 | Fat: 32g | Protein: 19g | Sodium: 74mg | Fiber: 1g | Carbohydrates: 3g

Coconut Beef Stir-Fry

This spicy dish will add a savory kick to any afternoon meal! For less heat, reduce the amount of chili powder and crushed red pepper.

INGREDIENTS | SERVES 6

1 pound flank steak

1 tablespoon ground turmeric

1 tablespoon chili powder

2 tablespoons coconut oil, melted and divided

1 teaspoon dark sesame oil

2 tablespoons fresh ginger, minced

3 cloves garlic, minced

1 onion, halved and sliced

¼ cup coconut milk

¼ cup fresh cilantro, chopped

½ teaspoon dried crushed red pepper

Turmeric

Turmeric is one of the most powerful antioxidants available and has many medicinal uses as well. Not only is it an antioxidant, it has anti-inflammatory properties. Curcumin, the active ingredient in turmeric, has been shown to be effective in helping treat Alzheimer's disease and is used in folk remedies in many parts of the world to treat several other medical conditions.

1. Cut steak diagonally across grain to maximize tenderness. Slice thinly into approximately ⅛" slices; season with turmeric and chili powder. Cover and chill for about 30 minutes.

2. Put 1 tablespoon of coconut oil into a heavy-bottomed skillet over medium-high heat. Add steak; stir-fry until browned. Remove from heat and sprinkle with sesame oil; toss to coat. Remove from skillet and set aside.

3. Put remaining 1 tablespoon of coconut oil into the skillet. Add ginger, garlic, and onion; stir-fry until onion is translucent.

4. Stir in coconut milk; cook, stirring constantly, for 2–3 minutes, or until sauce coats the spoon.

5. Stir in steak, cilantro, and red pepper. Cook for another minute, or until heated through. Serve over rice.

PER SERVING Calories: 192 | Fat: 12g | Protein: 17g | Sodium: 56mg | Fiber: 1g | Carbohydrates: 4g

Coconut Braised Beef

This tender beef dish with caramel-colored sauce makes a delicious addition to any menu!

INGREDIENTS | SERVES 6

2 hot dried red chilies
3 cloves garlic, minced
1 (1"-piece) ginger, grated
1 tablespoon chili powder
Juice and zest of 2 limes
2 tablespoons coconut oil
2 pounds stewing beef
1 (13.5-ounce) can coconut milk
Sea salt, to taste

1. In a food processor, place chilies, garlic, ginger, chili powder, lime juice and zest; process until finely chopped.

2. In a heavy-bottomed skillet, heat oil over medium-high heat. Add spice paste from the food processor; cook, stirring occasionally, for about 2 minutes.

3. Add stewing beef to skillet; cook for about 5 minutes, or until browned.

4. Pour in coconut milk; bring mixture to a boil. Reduce heat to low and cover; allow mixture to simmer, stirring occasionally, for about 1½ hours, or until meat is extremely tender.

5. Remove lid and cook for another 10–15 minutes, stirring frequently, until sauce is thick and caramel colored. Add salt, and serve with rice.

PER SERVING Calories: 365 | Fat: 24g | Protein: 33g | Sodium: 102mg | Fiber: 1g | Carbohydrates: 4g

Coconut Beef Curry

This exotic beef curry with its Eastern spice blend makes an easy one-dish meal.

INGREDIENTS | SERVES 6

1 tablespoon coconut oil

2 pounds stewing beef, cut into ¼" strips

2 onions, sliced

2 cloves garlic, minced

2 tablespoons paprika

2 tablespoons ground cumin

1 teaspoon cinnamon

1 tablespoon curry powder

4 medium potatoes, peeled and cubed

1 pound baby carrots, peeled

2 tablespoons tomato paste

1 (13.5-ounce) can coconut milk

½ cup water

1 teaspoon sea salt

Fresh cilantro, chopped, to taste

1. In a large skillet over medium-high heat, add coconut oil. Add beef strips; cook for 2–3 minutes, or until browned.

2. Add onions, garlic, paprika, cumin, cinnamon, and curry powder; sauté for 2 minutes.

3. With a slotted spoon, transfer beef mixture to a 6-quart slow cooker; add potatoes and carrots.

4. In a small bowl, combine tomato paste, coconut milk, water, and sea salt until well mixed. Add mixture to slow cooker with meat and vegetables.

5. Cover and cook on low heat for 8–10 hours, until vegetables are tender.

6. Sprinkle with fresh cilantro, and serve while still hot.

PER SERVING Calories: 538 | Fat: 28g | Protein: 37g | Sodium: 544mg | Fiber: 7g | Carbohydrates: 39g

Coconut Beef Stroganoff

This dairy-free version of the traditional beef stroganoff is sure to become a family favorite. For a gluten-free version, you can use quinoa or buckwheat pasta.

INGREDIENTS | SERVES 6

4 tablespoons coconut oil, divided

3 cloves garlic, minced

1 large onion, chopped

2 pounds beef chuck roast, cut into strips

Sea salt and pepper, to taste

1 pound fresh portobello mushrooms, chopped

2 tablespoons coconut vinegar

½ cup beef stock

1 tablespoon Worcestershire sauce

1 tablespoon tapioca starch

1 cup Coconut Sour Cream (see Chapter 20)

½ cup fresh parsley, chopped

Cultured Coconut Milk

If you have sensitivities to dairy, you can make a delicious nondairy sour cream. Use plain coconut milk yogurt and then strain out the excess liquid by pouring the yogurt through several layers of cheesecloth.

1. In a medium skillet, heat 3 tablespoons of coconut oil. Add garlic and onion; sauté for 2 minutes, or until onion begins to brown.

2. Grease the ceramic pot of your 6-quart slow cooker with additional coconut oil. Add beef strips to slow cooker, and salt and pepper to taste. Place onions and garlic in the slow cooker with the beef strips, then add the mushrooms.

3. In a small bowl, mix vinegar, beef stock, Worcestershire sauce, and tapioca starch; pour over the contents of the slow cooker. Cover and cook on low for 4–6 hours.

4. When beef is tender, just before serving, stir in Coconut Sour Cream (see Chapter 20) and chopped parsley. Serve over pasta.

PER SERVING Calories: 535 | Fat: 41g | Protein: 29g | Sodium: 194mg | Fiber: 2g | Carbohydrates: 13g

Coconut-Lime Hawaiian Pulled Pork

This succulent pulled pork recipe is complemented by a fabulous side of coconut grilled pineapple and is great served hot with Coconut Rice (see Chapter 15).

INGREDIENTS | SERVES 6

3 pound boneless pork roast
3 cloves garlic, sliced
1" piece fresh ginger, thinly sliced
Zest and juice from 2 limes
1 tablespoon sea salt
1 teaspoon garlic powder
2 tablespoons coconut oil, melted
1 pound fresh banana leaves
½ cup coconut milk
½ cup unrefined coconut sugar
1 fresh pineapple, cut into spears

Banana Leaves

Banana leaves are used as a wrapping in Asian and Hawaiian cooking. Not only do they serve to protect food from scorching and keep juices in, they also add subtle flavors that you will not get by using foil. Banana leaves can be found fresh or frozen in Asian markets. If you are unable to find banana leaves, kale leaves can be substituted.

1. Preheat the oven to 450°F.

2. Cut several slits into the roast at 1" intervals with a sharp knife. Insert garlic, ginger slices, and lime zest into each opening

3. In a small bowl, mix lime juice, salt, garlic powder, and coconut oil. Using a basting brush, spread mixture evenly over the entire pork roast.

4. Wrap entire roast with banana leaves and secure with hemp twine. Wrap roast in foil, and place in oven in a large roasting pan.

5. Add about 1" of water to the bottom of the roasting pan; roast for ½ hour.

6. Reduce heat to 400°F; roast for another 3–4 hours, until meat can easily be separated with a fork, adding water as needed to keep about 1" of water in the roasting pan at all times.

7. In a small bowl, mix coconut milk and sugar. Using a basting brush, coat pineapple evenly with mixture. Grill pineapple spears, basting occasionally with mixture, for about 2 minutes on each side, or until heated through and the sugar mixture begins to caramelize, turning slightly brown on the edges. Remove from grill and set aside.

Coconut-Lime Hawaiian Pulled Pork

(continued)

8. Remove roast from oven and let stand for about 10 minutes; transfer the roast to a baking dish, leaving the wrapping intact. Remove twine and wrapping and discard. Shred pork and combine with pan juices. Serve with grilled pineapple and Coconut Rice (see Chapter 15).

PER SERVING Calories: 556 | Fat: 22g | Protein: 52g | Sodium: 1277mg | Fiber: 0g | Carbohydrates: 38g

Sweet and Sour Pork with Coconut Sauce

This adobo sweet and sour pork recipe from the Philippines is a delicious alternative to the more common breaded version served in restaurants.

INGREDIENTS | SERVES 6

1 clove garlic, crushed

1 teaspoon paprika

1 teaspoon cracked black pepper

1 tablespoon raw coconut sugar

¾ cup coconut vinegar

2 bay leaves

2 pounds lean pork, cut into bite-sized pieces

2 cups chicken stock

½ cup creamed coconut

1 cucumber, peeled and diced

2 firm tomatoes, chopped

1 small bunch chives, chopped

2 tablespoons coconut oil

1 underripe papaya, peeled, seeded, and roughly chopped

Sea salt, to taste

1. In a resealable plastic bag, mix garlic, paprika, black pepper, coconut sugar, vinegar, and bay leaves. Add pork; marinate for at least 2 hours.

2. In a large skillet, mix chicken stock and creamed coconut. Add pork; simmer for about ½ hour. Remove pork and coconut sauce from skillet and set aside.

3. In a bowl, mix cucumber, tomatoes, and chives. Set aside.

4. Add coconut oil to hot skillet; return pork to the pan. Cook for another 2–3 minutes, or until browned.

5. Add coconut sauce back to the skillet with pork. Add papaya and sea salt; cook, covered, for another 10–15 minutes. Top with cucumber mixture, and serve.

PER SERVING Calories: 396 | Fat: 20g | Protein: 32g | Sodium: 299mg | Fiber: 2g | Carbohydrates: 22g

Indian Coconut Lamb Curry

Indian curry recipes have a long list of ingredients, but are surprisingly easy to make! This Indian Coconut Lamb Curry is done in three easy steps.

INGREDIENTS | SERVES 6

⅓ cup cashews, roughly chopped

2 cloves garlic, minced

½ teaspoon chili powder

1 heaping tablespoon fresh ginger, grated

½ teaspoon ground coriander

½ teaspoon turmeric

1 teaspoon fresh cilantro, chopped

½ teaspoon garam masala

½ teaspoon ground pepper

½ cup coconut ghee

1 small onion, diced

2 pounds lamb

1 cup coconut milk

¼ teaspoon saffron powder

¼ cup golden raisins

½ teaspoon sea salt

½ cup slivered almonds

6 sweet neem leaves, crumbled

1. In a food processor, blend cashews, garlic, chili powder, ginger, coriander, turmeric, cilantro, garam masala, and pepper.

2. In a large skillet, add ghee and onion; cook on medium heat for 2–3 minutes, or until onions become translucent. Add spice mixture from the food processor and continue to cook for another 5 minutes.

3. Cut meat into 1" cubes. Add to the skillet and cook until browned, about 5 minutes.

4. Add coconut milk, saffron, raisins, and salt; cover and cook on low heat for about 1 hour, or until meat is tender and sauce is thickened. Remove from heat and add almonds and neem leaves to serve.

PER SERVING Calories: 633 | Fat: 52g | Protein: 33g | Sodium: 291mg | Fiber: 2g | Carbohydrates: 13g

Garam Masala

Like curry, garam masala is a blend of spices commonly used in Indian and south Asian cuisine. Garam masala usually contains a blend of toasted cloves, cardamom, coriander, anise, and malabar leaves that have been previously toasted. This can be combined with ground nuts, onions, or garlic to make a paste or used as a powder.

Coconut Meatballs

These delicious meatballs fried in coconut oil are served with rice and a yummy coconut mushroom sauce.

INGREDIENTS | SERVES 6

2 pounds ground beef

1 large onion, diced

2 cloves garlic, pressed

2 eggs

½ teaspoon sea salt

1 teaspoon ground cumin

1 teaspoon coriander

¼ teaspoon cayenne

½ teaspoon oyster sauce

1 cup coconut milk, divided

3 tablespoons coconut oil

½ cup portobello mushrooms, chopped

1 teaspoon potato starch flour

1 tablespoon cold water

Fresh cilantro, chopped, to taste

Coconut Milk, Coconut Cream, and Creamed Coconut

When working with coconut recipes, it can be confusing when you see ingredients like coconut cream, coconut milk, coconut water, and creamed coconut. Each of these ingredients is different, but unless you work with coconut recipes a lot, you might not know the difference. Coconut water is the clear liquid inside the coconut. Coconut milk is made by blending the coconut meat with water and then straining out the "milk." The coconut cream will rise to the top of the coconut milk and can be skimmed off, much like cream from fresh whole cow's milk. To make cream of coconut, strain the liquid out of the coconut cream by passing it through several layers of cheesecloth or a fine sieve.

1. In a bowl, combine ground beef, onion, garlic, egg, salt, cumin, coriander, cayenne, oyster sauce, and 4 tablespoons of coconut milk until well mixed. Shape into 1" balls.

2. In a heavy-bottomed skillet, heat the coconut oil and cook the meatballs until browned, about 5 minutes.

3. Remove meatballs from the skillet and add mushrooms. Cook for 2–3 minutes, then add remaining coconut milk. Stir, scraping the bottom of the skillet to loosen meat juices from the bottom of the pan.

4. In a small bowl, mix the potato starch flour and cold water. Whisk into coconut milk mixture; bring to a simmer. Cook for another 2–3 minutes, or until sauce begins to thicken.

5. Serve meatballs with rice and top with coconut mushroom sauce and cilantro.

PER SERVING Calories: 515 | Fat: 42g | Protein: 29g | Sodium: 323mg | Fiber: 1g | Carbohydrates: 5g

Kalio Hati (Malaysian Liver in Coconut Milk)

Try this Malaysian twist on liver and onions for a nutrient-dense energy booster.

INGREDIENTS | SERVES 6

1 small onion, chopped

3 cloves garlic

6 bird's eye chilies, sliced

1" fresh galangal, peeled and sliced

1" fresh turmeric, peeled and sliced

1" fresh ginger, peeled and sliced

2 tablespoons coconut oil

1 lemongrass stalk, bruised

1 medium onion, sliced

2 sweet neem leaves

1½ pounds beef liver, sliced into strips

3 cups coconut milk

1 teaspoon sea salt

Galangal

Galangal is a root spice in the ginger family, and is often used as a complement to ginger in many Asian recipes. Fresh galangal root is much harder than ginger, and requires a sharp knife for cutting. In recipes that call for crushed galangal, the galangal will need to be cut into strips first before crushing.

1. To prepare the curry paste, in a food processor, add onion, garlic, chilies, galangal, turmeric, and ginger and process until smooth.

2. Heat coconut oil in a wok. Add curry paste, lemongrass, onion, and neem leaves; cook for about 2 minutes.

3. Add liver; sauté until browned, about 3–5 minutes.

4. Add coconut milk and salt; simmer uncovered for another 10 minutes, or until liver is tender and sauce has thickened. Serve with side bowls of Coconut Rice (see Chapter 15).

PER SERVING Calories: 449 | Fat: 33g | Protein: 27g | Sodium: 485mg | Fiber: 1g | Carbohydrates: 16g

Chicken Satay with Peanut Coconut Sauce

Thai peanut sauce is surprisingly savory and not at all like peanut butter as some people might expect. This spicy coconut peanut sauce is fantastic with broiled chicken.

INGREDIENTS | SERVES 6

1 (13.5-ounce) can coconut milk

3 tablespoons creamy peanut butter

2 tablespoons fresh lime juice

2 tablespoons curry paste

3 tablespoons raw coconut sugar

1 teaspoon fresh ginger, grated

2 cloves garlic, minced

½ teaspoon red pepper flakes

2 pounds boneless, skinless chicken breasts

Peanut Sauce

Sauces made with peanuts are very popular in many Asian countries and in Africa. However, they are not known as peanut sauce; rather, the sauces contain peanuts as an ingredient. In traditional sauces that contain peanuts, the peanuts are often coarsely ground to add texture and are not usually a main ingredient in the sauce itself.

1. In a food processor, mix coconut milk, peanut butter, lime juice, curry paste, coconut sugar, ginger, garlic, and red pepper flakes. Remove ¼ of the sauce and set aside.

2. Cut chicken into 1" cubes; use reserved peanut sauce as a marinade. Allow chicken to marinate for at least 1 hour.

3. Using 6 wooden skewers, thread about 7 cubes of chicken on each skewer; lay them on a broiler pan. Cook skewers under the broiler, turning occasionally, for about 6–8 minutes, or until chicken is cooked through and browned.

4. Serve chicken with peanut coconut dipping sauce and a cucumber salad on the side.

PER SERVING Calories: 318 | Fat: 15g | Protein: 37g | Sodium: 133mg | Fiber: 1g | Carbohydrates: 9g

Spare Ribs with Honey Coconut Glaze

These yummy baked spare ribs are perfect for a backyard picnic. The unique barbecue flavor with an Eastern flair lends itself well to either a side of rice or a side of Coconut Garlic Roasted Cowboy Fries (see Chapter 15).

INGREDIENTS | SERVES 8

½ cup soy sauce
¼ cup coconut milk
1 bunch green onions, finely chopped
3 tablespoons fresh ginger, grated
8 cloves garlic, pressed
½ cup raw coconut sugar
1 tablespoon curry powder
⅔ cup raw honey
¼ cup fresh orange juice
¼ cup fresh lemon juice
2 tablespoons Dijon-style mustard
1 tablespoon sesame oil
4 pounds spare ribs

1. Preheat the oven to 350°F.

2. In a food processor, mix soy sauce, coconut milk, green onions, ginger, garlic, coconut sugar, curry, honey, orange juice, lemon juice, mustard, and sesame oil.

3. Place the ribs in a large baking pan; pour the sauce mixture over the ribs, coating evenly. Cover the ribs with foil; bake for 1 hour.

4. Remove from oven and serve with Coconut Garlic Roasted Cowboy Fries (see Chapter 15) or over rice.

PER SERVING Calories: 1082 | Fat: 75g | Protein: 49g | Sodium: 1503mg | Fiber: 1g | Carbohydrates: 55g

Slow-Cooked Coconut Shredded-Beef Taco Filling

Try this shredded taco mix slow cooked in salsa and coconut milk with soft Coconut Flour Tortillas/Crepes (see Chapter 17).

INGREDIENTS | SERVES 6

1 cup medium salsa
4 cloves garlic, pressed
½ cup coconut milk
2 pounds stew beef
2 ripe tomatoes, diced
1 ripe avocado, diced
¼ cup fresh cilantro, chopped
1 tablespoon fresh lime juice

Cilantro

Cilantro is the Spanish word for coriander leaves, but the two are not necessarily interchangeable. Cilantro, or the coriander plant, is very popular in South American recipes as well as Eastern recipes, especially in India. In recipes that call for cilantro, it is generally referring to the fresh leaves of the coriander plant, but if the recipe calls for coriander, unless it specifies fresh coriander leaves, it is usually referring to ground coriander seed. Dried coriander leaves have little to no flavor, while ground coriander seed is very flavorful.

1. In a bowl, mix salsa, garlic, coconut milk, and beef. Pour into a 6-quart slow cooker, cover, and cook for 6–8 hours on low heat, or until meat can be shredded with a fork.

2. In a small serving bowl, mix diced tomatoes and avocado; set aside.

3. Shred meat with 2 forks; stir in cilantro and lime juice. Serve with Coconut Flour Tortillas/Crepes (see Chapter 17), diced tomatoes and avocados, and Coconut Sour Cream (see Chapter 20).

PER SERVING Calories: 490 | Fat: 38g | Protein: 28g | Sodium: 271mg | Fiber: 3g | Carbohydrates: 9g

Slow Cooker Coconut Beef Curry

This easy coconut beef curry recipe is a great way to get started making Eastern-style curry recipes. Toss your ingredients in the slow cooker, and eat a few hours later!

INGREDIENTS | SERVES 8

1 tablespoon coconut oil

1 (2-pound) pot roast

2 large onions, quartered

1 (13.5-ounce) can coconut milk

2 cloves garlic, minced

2 tablespoons fresh ginger, grated

2 teaspoons curry powder

1 tablespoon ground coriander seed

1 tablespoon chili pepper flakes

Salt and pepper, to taste

1. In a large, hot skillet, melt coconut oil. Brown beef on high heat until seared on all sides, about 2–3 minutes. Remove meat from skillet and transfer into the slow cooker with onions.

2. In a bowl, mix coconut milk, garlic, ginger, curry, coriander, chili pepper, salt, and pepper; pour over meat. Cook on low heat for 6–8 hours.

PER SERVING Calories: 407 | Fat: 32g | Protein: 23g | Sodium: 79mg | Fiber: 1g | Carbohydrates: 6g |

CHAPTER 14

Fish and Seafood

Moqueca (Brazilian Fish Stew)

This delicious fish stew made with a coconut base is a popular dish in Brazil. Add some warm crusty bread and butter, and you have the ultimate comfort food! This can also be made with salmon.

INGREDIENTS | SERVES 6

3 pounds halibut fillets

6 cloves garlic, minced

½ cup lime juice

1 teaspoon sea salt plus additional salt, to taste

Freshly ground black pepper, to taste

3 tablespoons coconut oil

2 medium white onions, chopped

2 cups uncooked white rice

2 cups water

2 (14-ounce) cans coconut milk

1 yellow bell pepper, sliced

1 red bell pepper, sliced

1½ teaspoons ground cumin

¼ teaspoon red pepper flakes

2 cups tomatoes, diced

¼ cup green onions, chopped

1 large bunch fresh cilantro, chopped, 6 sprigs reserved for garnish

1. Rinse halibut in cold water and cut into 6 portions. Place pieces in a bowl.

2. Combine 4 cloves of minced garlic and lime juice; mix well. Pour over halibut, making sure all pieces of fish are well coated. Add salt and pepper, to taste. Cover and keep in the refrigerator.

3. In a medium saucepan over medium heat, melt 2 tablespoons of coconut oil. Add 1 chopped onion and remaining garlic. Sauté for 3 minutes, or until the onion is translucent.

4. Add uncooked white rice and stir to coat. Add water, 2 cups coconut milk, and 1 teaspoon of sea salt; stir and cook on medium-high heat for about 5 minutes, or until rice comes to a boil. Once rice is boiling, cover and reduce to low heat; cook for another 15 minutes. Remove from heat.

5. In a large pot over medium-high heat, melt the remaining coconut oil. Add the second chopped onion; sauté for 3 minutes, until onion is translucent.

6. Add bell peppers, cumin, red pepper flakes, and salt and pepper, to taste. Cook another 3 minutes, or until bell peppers begin to soften; add tomatoes and green onions. Bring to a simmer and cook, uncovered, for another 5 minutes.

7. Stir in chopped cilantro; use a large slotted spoon to remove half of the vegetables to a bowl. Set aside.

Moqueca (Brazilian Fish Stew)

(continued)

8. Spread the remaining vegetables evenly over the bottom of the pot. Arrange halibut portions on top of the vegetables; return removed vegetables to the pot, covering the pieces of fish.

9. Pour remaining coconut milk over all; cook on medium heat, about 5 minutes, until stew comes to a simmer. Reduce heat to medium low; cover and let simmer for another 15 minutes. Garnish with remaining cilantro sprigs, and serve with rice.

PER SERVING Calories: 837 | Fat: 41g | Protein: 55g | Sodium: 540mg | Fiber: 3g | Carbohydrates: 65g

Curried Cod with Coconut Milk

Fish curries are very popular and easy to make. This sauce has a creamy coconut and tomato base.

INGREDIENTS | SERVES 6

1 tablespoon coconut flour
1 tablespoon turmeric
3 pounds cod
2 tablespoons coconut oil
1 medium white onion, minced
1 tablespoon curry powder
⅓ cup tomato sauce
1 (14-ounce) can coconut milk
Sea salt and pepper, to taste
1 tablespoon fresh cilantro, minced

White Ocean Fish

White ocean fish like cod, halibut, and herring are usually low in mercury and safe to eat. When possible, get wild-caught fish from cold-water regions or fish that were farmed in the United States. Cold-water fish farmed in warmer regions absorb more toxins from the water, so especially avoid eating any type of fish that has been farmed in warmer regions where there is more pollution in the water.

1. In a large shallow bowl, combine coconut flour and turmeric. Dip each piece of cod in the coconut flour mixture. Cover and store in the refrigerator.

2. In a large skillet over medium-high heat, add oil and chopped onion; sauté onion for about 3 minutes, or until translucent.

3. Add curry powder, tomato sauce, and coconut milk; stir. Add salt and pepper, to taste; cook another 5 minutes.

4. Add the cod to the skillet; cook, covered, for about 5 minutes. Remove cod to a serving plate, cover with sauce, and sprinkle with cilantro. Serve hot.

PER SERVING Calories: 376 | Fat: 20g | Protein: 42g | Sodium: 204mg | Fiber: 2g | Carbohydrates: 7g

Grilled Cilantro Tilapia in Coconut Broth

Grilled tilapia fillets go wonderfully with this creamy coconut sauce, but you could also use any other firm white-fish fillets, as well.

INGREDIENTS | SERVES 6

Coconut oil as needed for the grill plus 2 tablespoons

½ cup fresh cilantro

1 clove garlic, minced

Juice of 2 limes, divided

Sea salt, to taste

¼ teaspoon red pepper flakes

3 pounds tilapia fillets

2 tablespoons green onion, minced

2 tablespoons fresh ginger, grated

Zest of 1 lime

3 cups coconut milk

1 Serrano chili pepper, seeded and chopped

1. Brush grill with coconut oil and heat to medium-high.

2. In a food processor, mix cilantro, garlic, juice from 1 lime, sea salt, red pepper, and 1 tablespoon of melted coconut oil. Place tilapia fillets in a shallow bowl and pour spice mixture over fish, coating evenly. Allow to marinate for about 15 minutes.

3. In a large skillet over medium-high heat, use remaining coconut oil to sauté green onions, ginger, and lime zest until soft, about 3 minutes.

4. Add coconut milk and remaining lime juice. Bring to a simmer; cook broth for about 2 minutes. Stir in chili pepper; reduce heat to low.

5. Remove fish from marinade; discard excess marinade. Grill fish, covered, for about 5 minutes on one side; turn and grill another 5 minutes, or until fish is firm and flakes easily. Divide broth between 6 bowls, add fish, and serve hot.

PER SERVING Calories: 483 | Fat: 32g | Protein: 48g | Sodium: 133mg | Fiber: 0g | Carbohydrates: 5g

Seared Tuna Salad with Coconut Lime Dressing

This fresh seared-tuna salad is absolutely delicious! Crunchy tortilla strips fried in coconut oil, freshly cooked tuna steak, greens, and a zesty coconut lime dressing make a wonderful combination!

INGREDIENTS | SERVES 6

4 (6") corn tortillas, cut into ¼" strips
1 teaspoon ground cumin
1½ teaspoons sea salt, divided
¼ teaspoon red pepper flakes
2 tablespoons coconut oil, divided
3 pounds tuna steak
½ teaspoon freshly ground black pepper
1 (14-ounce) can coconut milk
Juice of 2 limes
2 teaspoons fish sauce
2 teaspoons raw coconut sugar
6 cups mixed salad greens
1 cup grape tomatoes, halved
¼ cup red onion, thinly sliced
1 avocado, pitted, peeled, and sliced

Fresh Tuna

If you are buying fresh tuna, you want to get it directly from a fishmonger or from a grocery store with a good reputation. Fish should have a fresh ocean smell or no smell at all. It should not have a strong, fishy smell. The skin should be wet, not dry, and the flesh should be firm, not mushy. There are a lot of concerns about eating tuna lately because of high levels of mercury found in canned tuna samples. If you stick with wild tuna caught in cold-water regions of the Pacific Northwest, you will not need to worry about high mercury levels in your tuna.

1. In a small bowl, mix tortilla strips, cumin, ½ teaspoon salt, and red pepper flakes; toss to coat tortilla strips.

2. In a large skillet, melt 1 tablespoon coconut oil. Add the tortilla strips; cook 3–5 minutes, stirring occasionally, until golden. Remove tortilla strips from skillet and set aside.

3. Sprinkle tuna with black pepper and remaining teaspoon of sea salt. Add remaining coconut oil and tuna to skillet. Cook tuna for about 5 minutes on medium-high heat; turn and cook another 5 minutes. Cut into ½" strips.

4. In a small bowl, whisk together the coconut milk, lime juice, fish sauce, and coconut sugar to make a coconut milk dressing.

5. In a large serving bowl, mix greens, tomatoes, and red onion. Add ½ cup of the coconut milk dressing; toss to coat.

6. Divide salad evenly among 6 serving plates; top evenly with tuna, avocado, and fried tortilla strips. Serve with remaining dressing on the side.

PER SERVING Calories: 594 | Fat: 35g | Protein: 56g | Sodium: 849mg | Fiber: 4g | Carbohydrates: 15g

Jamaican Coconut Red Snapper

This delightful twist on the classic beer-batter fish and chips takes advantage of the high-temperature properties of coconut oil for frying.

INGREDIENTS | SERVES 6

⅔ cup coconut flour

1 cup teff flour

⅓ cup potato starch

2 teaspoons baking powder

4 large eggs

1 (12-ounce) can beer

1 large yellow onion

½ cup coconut oil for frying

3 cups grated fresh coconut

2 pounds red snapper fillets

Sea salt and pepper, to taste

1. In a bowl, mix coconut flour, teff flour, and potato starch. Mix well and remove ½ cup to a shallow dish; set aside. Add baking powder to the flour mixture in the bowl; mix well. Make an indentation in the center and add eggs and beer; mix well.

2. Slice onion into ½" slices, separating them out into individual rings.

3. Dip onion rings into just the beer batter and fry onions in batches until golden brown and onions are soft, about 3 minutes on each side. Drain on paper towels. Cover and set aside.

4. In a second shallow bowl, place grated coconut.

5. Arrange bowls so that the dish with the flour is first, the bowl with the batter is in the middle, and the dish with the shredded coconut is third. Place an empty plate at the end to hold the battered fillets.

6. Season the snapper fillets with the salt and pepper and lightly dredge each snapper fillet in flour, then dip in beer batter, and coat with shredded coconut. Repeat until all of the snapper fillets are coated.

7. In a large skillet, heat coconut oil again and fry each fillet until golden brown, about 2 minutes on each side. Drain on a plate lined with paper towels and serve with onion rings.

PER SERVING Calories: 608 | Fat: 36g | Protein: 20g | Sodium: 849mg | Fiber: 4g | Carbohydrates: 15g

Thai Fish in Banana Leaf

These quaint banana leaf "packages" of seasoned steamed fish make a lovely presentation for entertaining, and take advantage of the distinctive Thai flavors of lemongrass and curry.

INGREDIENTS | SERVES 6

1 tablespoon red curry paste

⅓ cup coconut milk

2 eggs

3 tablespoons lemongrass, finely chopped

¼ cup fish sauce

3 tablespoons fresh basil, minced, plus a few leaves for garnish

1 teaspoon fresh dill, chopped

6 sweet neem leaves, finely chopped

¼ cup onion, minced

2 tablespoons rice flour

2 pounds cod fillets

2 pounds banana leaves

Cilantro, for garnish

Sweet Neem Leaves

Sweet neem leaves are also known as curry leaves. Even though the plant itself is not curry, the leaves are often called curry leaves because they are commonly used for making curry powder or curry pastes.

1. In a bowl, mix curry paste, coconut milk, and eggs; add lemongrass, fish sauce, basil, dill, neem leaves, onion, and rice flour. Add mixture to a resealable plastic bag with cod fillets. Squeeze gently to coat fish; put in the refrigerator to marinate for about 15 minutes.

2. Spread out one banana leaf, at least 1-foot square. Place one cod fillet in the middle of the banana leaf and fold around the fish to make a square package. Wrap securely in foil; repeat the process for each cod fillet.

3. In a glass baking pan big enough to fit fillets, place foil-wrapped packages together; bake for 10 minutes. Remove one packet and check the fish. If it is done, the fish will flake easily with a fork and the flesh will be opaque and white in color. If the fish is not done, return it to the oven and cook for another 10 minutes. Remove from the oven; serve with Coconut Rice (see Chapter 15), and garnish with basil and cilantro.

PER SERVING Calories: 196 | Fat: 6g | Protein: 30g | Sodium: 1033mg | Fiber: 1g | Carbohydrates: 5g

Baked Salmon with Coconut Crust

Baked salmon makes a nice sit-down meal in a short amount of time. The combination of omega-3 fatty acids in the salmon are complemented by the healthy qualities of the coconut oil.

INGREDIENTS | SERVES 6

1 (3-pound) salmon fillet
1 tablespoon coconut oil
2 tablespoons lemon juice
½ cup dry bread crumbs
Sea salt and freshly ground black pepper, to taste
1 cup grated coconut

Buying Salmon

Farmed or wild? The difference is not just the price. Farmed salmon are fed fish pellets that usually contain antibiotics as opposed to their natural diet, which would normally consist of krill and other natural foods. Farmed salmon are raised in crowded conditions and are more prone to infection and mercury contamination. Because of their artificial diet, they also have less beneficial omega-3s and other nutrients.

1. Preheat the oven to 400°F.

2. Cut salmon fillet into 6 equal pieces; place on parchment-lined baking sheet.

3. Melt coconut oil; mix with lemon juice. Use a basting brush to coat salmon pieces.

4. Mix bread crumbs, salt, pepper, and coconut.

5. Dip each piece of salmon in the coconut mixture; return to baking sheet. Sprinkle any remaining coconut topping over salmon pieces; bake for 15 minutes. Serve hot.

PER SERVING Calories: 394 | Fat: 18g | Protein: 47g | Sodium: 220mg | Fiber: 2g | Carbohydrates: 10g

Steelhead Trout with Coconut Cream Sauce

Steelhead trout is very similar to salmon. If you are unable to find steelhead at your supermarket, you can use salmon as a substitute in this recipe.

INGREDIENTS | SERVES 6

2 tablespoons coconut oil
2 tablespoons chives, chopped
3 cloves garlic, minced
2 tablespoons anchovy paste
Sea salt and pepper, to taste
1 (3-pound) steelhead trout fillet
1 cup coconut milk
1 tablespoon chili sauce
2 tablespoons fresh ginger, grated
Juice of 1 large orange
Juice of 1 lime
½ cup coconut cream
2 tablespoons cilantro, chopped

1. In a medium bowl, mix 1 tablespoon warmed coconut oil, chives, garlic, 1 tablespoon anchovy paste, and salt and pepper. Using a basting brush, evenly coat steelhead. Cover and let sit refrigerated for 10–15 minutes.

2. In a large skillet on medium-high, melt remaining coconut oil. Add coconut milk, chili sauce, ginger, orange juice, and lime juice. Simmer on medium-low heat for about 10–15 minutes, or until reduced by half. Remove from heat; stir in coconut cream.

3. Place steelhead on a broiler rack; place under the broiler for 5 minutes. Remove from oven and carefully turn. Broil for another 3–5 minutes, or until cooked through. Serve with coconut cream sauce, and sprinkle with fresh cilantro.

PER SERVING Calories: 549 | Fat: 32g | Protein: 48g | Sodium: 169mg | Fiber: 0g | Carbohydrates: 18g

Coconut Herrings

These fresh coconut-crusted herrings are packed with omega-3s! This small fish is tasty and good for you.

INGREDIENTS | SERVES 6

¼ cup coconut flour

1 teaspoon garlic powder

Sea salt and freshly ground black pepper, to taste

2 eggs, beaten

⅓ cup grated fresh coconut

24 herring fillets, large pin bones removed, about 3 pounds

¼ cup coconut oil

1 (12-ounce) jar mango salsa

Herrings

Herrings have some of the highest levels of omega-3 fatty acids of any other type of fish. Herrings contain up to 2 grams of omega-3 fats for every 3 ounces of fish! Herrings are not just canned, pickled fish. Fresh herrings are hard to find, but if you live near a fish market, they are definitely worth watching for.

1. In a shallow dish, combine coconut flour, garlic powder, salt, and pepper.

2. In a second shallow dish, beat eggs; set aside.

3. In a third shallow dish, place grated coconut.

4. Dredge fillets in flour mixture, dip in eggs, and then coat in coconut; set aside. Repeat with each fillet.

5. Heat coconut oil in a large skillet. When oil is hot enough for frying, place herring fillets in skillet a few at a time; fry until golden brown, about 2 minutes on each side. Remove from skillet and place on a paper-towel-lined plate to drain. Serve hot, with Coconut Rice (see Chapter 15) and mango salsa.

PER SERVING Calories: 613 | Fat: 44g | Protein: 40g | Sodium: 191mg | Fiber: 3g | Carbohydrates: 146

Coconut-Crumbed Mahi-Mahi Fillet

Hawaiian mahi-mahi with homemade mango salsa is a heavenly way to get more fish in your diet. Combine this with coconut, and you have a winning combination!

INGREDIENTS | SERVES 6

2 mangoes, peeled and cubed
2 tablespoons fresh basil, chopped
3 cloves garlic, chopped
½ teaspoon freshly ground black pepper
½ cup coconut flour
2 eggs, beaten
1 cup shredded fresh coconut
2 pounds mahi-mahi
½ cup coconut oil

Mahi-Mahi

Mahi-mahi, or dolphinfish, is not dolphin meat. Mahi-mahi is a tropical fish with pink flesh that comes from the Pacific Ocean near the Hawaiian Islands. It can be found fresh or frozen. If you are thawing frozen fish, it should be thawed overnight in the refrigerator or under cold running water. Mahi-mahi will last up to 4 months in your freezer.

1. In a food processor, mix mangos, basil, garlic, and black pepper. Pulse until all ingredients are roughly chopped and well mixed. Set aside.

2. In a shallow bowl, place coconut flour.

3. In a second shallow bowl, place eggs.

4. In a third shallow bowl, place coconut.

5. Dip mahi-mahi pieces in coconut flour, then in eggs, then coat with coconut. Chill for at least 1 hour.

6. In a large skillet, heat coconut oil until it is hot enough for frying. Fry fish for about 5 minutes on each side, until golden brown and cooked through. Serve with fresh mango salsa.

PER SERVING Calories: 507 | Fat: 31g | Protein: 37g | Sodium: 63mg | Fiber: 7g | Carbohydrates: 21g

Thai Seafood with Coconut Galangal Sauce

This delicious seafood dish combines the goodness of coconut milk with several powerful herbs and spices that will nourish your body and boost your immune system.

INGREDIENTS | SERVES 6

5 tablespoons coconut oil

1 clove garlic, chopped

2 small onions, chopped

1 tablespoon fresh lemongrass, chopped

1 tablespoon curry paste

1 tablespoon tamarind paste

1" piece fresh ginger, sliced

1" piece fresh galangal root, sliced

1 (14-ounce) can coconut milk

Juice of 1 lime

2 quarts water

1 pound shrimp, shelled and deveined

1 pound scallops

1 pound squid, cleaned and sliced

1 fresh red chili, sliced

2 tablespoons chili sauce

½ cup coconut cream

1 tablespoon fish sauce

Lemongrass

Lemongrass is native to the Philippines, and is a popular herb used in Thai, Vietnamese, and Indian cooking. Lemongrass is a powerful anticancer herb, and has been studied for its ability to kill cancer cells.

1. In a medium saucepan over medium heat, heat 4 tablespoons coconut oil, garlic, 1 onion, lemongrass, curry paste, tamarind paste, ginger, and galangal. Sauté for 5 minutes, then add coconut milk and lime juice. Bring to a boil and reduce heat to medium-low; let simmer for 3 minutes. Remove from heat.

2. In a medium pot, add 2 quarts of water and bring to a boil. Add seafood; blanch in boiling water for 1 minute. Drain and set aside.

3. Pour coconut galangal sauce mixture into a blender or food processor; blend until smooth.

4. In a wok over high heat, heat remaining tablespoon of coconut oil. Add remaining onion and red chili; stir-fry until onion is translucent, about 3 minutes. Add the shrimp, scallops, and squid; toss to mix. Pour coconut galangal sauce over seafood; add the chili sauce, coconut cream, and fish sauce. Cook in wok until seafood is cooked through, about 5–8 minutes. Serve with Coconut Rice (see Chapter 15).

PER SERVING Calories: 554 | Fat: 32g | Protein: 42g | Sodium: 520mg | Fiber: 1g | Carbohydrates: 25g

Hawaiian Coconut Shrimp

With a few small changes to the recipe, this coconut shrimp changes from a no-no full of trans fats and carbohydrates to an oh, yes! with low-carb coconut flour and heart-healthy coconut oil.

INGREDIENTS | SERVES 6

⅓ cup Dijon mustard

⅓ cup Coconut Sour Cream (see Chapter 20)

⅓ cup honey

1 teaspoon prepared horseradish

2 pounds large shrimp

¼ cup coconut flour, plus ⅓ cup, divided use

⅓ cup amaranth flour

⅓ cup potato starch flour

¾ teaspoon baking powder

¼ teaspoon sea salt

⅓ cup coconut milk

½ cup grated coconut

½ cup coconut oil

Amaranth

Amaranth is a gluten-free, high-protein grain that can be used in conjunction with coconut flour and other nongrain flours to improve the texture of baked goods and other recipes. Even if you are not intolerant to gluten, it is beneficial to eat a variety of grains and seeds. One of the common ways that allergies can develop is by eating the same foods day after day with no variation.

1. In a small bowl, mix mustard, coconut sour cream, honey, and horseradish. Cover and set aside.

2. Peel and devein shrimp, leaving tails intact.

3. In a small bowl, mix ¼ cup coconut flour, amaranth flour, potato starch flour, baking powder, salt, and coconut milk to form a batter. Place in a shallow dish.

4. In a second shallow dish, place ⅓ cup coconut flour.

5. In a third shallow dish, place grated coconut.

6. Take a shrimp by the tail; dip it in the flour, coating thoroughly with a light coat. Then dip in the batter, then in the coconut; set on a plate. Repeat the process with each shrimp. Cover shrimp and chill for 1 hour.

7. Heat coconut oil in a large skillet. Fry shrimp in batches for 2–3 minutes on each side, until golden brown. Remove from skillet and drain on a plate lined with paper towels. Serve with honey mustard sauce, to taste.

PER SERVING Calories: 557 | Fat: 29g | Protein: 34g | Sodium: 541mg | Fiber: 7g | Carbohydrates: 43g

Seafood Gumbo with Coconut Milk

This seafood gumbo brings together the best of Louisiana's soul food with the distinctive flavors of the Old South.

INGREDIENTS | SERVES 8

2 tablespoons coconut oil

1 small yellow onion, diced

1 small red bell pepper, diced

½ cup celery, diced

1 pound mustard greens, roughly chopped

2 small shallots, minced

2 tablespoons fresh ginger, grated

2 cloves garlic, minced

Zest of 1 lime

4 cups fish stock

1 (14-ounce) can coconut milk

½ habanero pepper

2 teaspoons fresh thyme, chopped

Juice of 2 limes

2 teaspoons sea salt

1 pound medium shrimp, peeled and deveined

1 pound red snapper fillet, cut into 1" pieces

½ pound calamari, sliced

¼ pound crabmeat, picked over

1 tablespoon plus 1 teaspoon Worcestershire sauce

1 tablespoon fresh parsley, chopped

1 tablespoon fresh cilantro, chopped

1. In a large soup pot on medium-high heat, heat coconut oil. Add onions, bell pepper, and celery; sauté for about 5 minutes, or until onions are translucent and the peppers and celery are tender. Add mustard greens; sauté another 2–3 minutes.

2. Add the shallots, ginger, garlic, and lime zest; cook for another minute to allow flavors to blend.

3. Add fish stock, coconut milk, habanero pepper, thyme, lime juice, and salt; raise the temperature to high.

4. Bring to a boil; reduce heat to medium and bring down to a simmer. Let simmer for 20 minutes.

5. Add the shrimp and red snapper; cook for another 5 minutes. Add calamari, crabmeat, Worcestershire sauce, parsley, and cilantro. Serve with rice.

PER SERVING Calories: 331 | Fat: 17g | Protein: 36g | Sodium: 1002mg | Fiber: 2g | Carbohydrates: 9g

Shallots

Shallots grow in clusters like garlic, and are milder and sweeter than onions. They are often used interchangeably with onions in recipes, but they don't have that obnoxious tendency to make you cry the way the onion does!

Coconut Curry Seafood Crepes

Ooh, la, la! These seafood crepes with their creamy coconut sauce are a great way to end the day. Try these with a side of Asparagus in Coconut Milk (see Chapter 15).

INGREDIENTS | SERVES 6

3 cups chicken broth

½ pound shrimp, peeled and deveined

½ pound salmon fillet

¼ cup coconut ghee

1 medium onion, diced

6 tablespoons whole-wheat pastry flour

1½ cups coconut milk

Sea salt and pepper, to taste

½ pound crabmeat

6 Coconut Flour Tortillas/Crepes (see Chapter 17)

Crab

Crab must be purchased either live or already cooked. The best way to make sure the crab is fresh is to boil it when it is still alive. Once a crab has died, it begins to go bad quickly, and you can get very sick from eating crab that was dead before cooking. Another reason for cooking crabs alive is that crabmeat is very soft. If you try to remove crabmeat from an uncooked crab, chances are you will end up wasting most of it. The meat firms up after being cooked and is then much easier to remove from the shell.

1. In a medium saucepan over high heat, bring chicken broth to a boil. Add shrimp; cover, and remove from heat. Let stand about 3 minutes; transfer to a cutting board with a slotted spoon.

2. Return pan to high heat and bring to a boil. Add salmon; cover, and remove from heat. Let stand about 10 minutes; transfer to the cutting board with the shrimp. Pour broth into a 4-cup measuring cup and rinse pan.

3. In a saucepan over medium-high heat, heat ghee. Add onion; cook for 10 minutes, or until onion is translucent and cooked through. Sprinkle with flour; stir until well mixed.

4. Whisk in reserved broth and coconut milk; continue to stir over medium heat for about 10 minutes, or until sauce comes to a boil. Remove from heat and add salt and pepper, to taste.

5. Cut shrimp and salmon into ½" cubes and add crabmeat. Mix in 1 cup of coconut sauce.

6. Preheat the oven to 350°F. Spoon about ¼ cup of seafood mixture onto a warm Coconut Flour Tortilla/Crepe (see Chapter 17). Roll crepes and lay in 9" × 13" glass baking pan greased with coconut oil or ghee.

7. Bake for about 45 minutes, or until cooked through. Serve with coconut sauce, and sprinkle with cilantro for garnish.

PER SERVING Calories: 395 | Fat: 27g | Protein: 28g | Sodium: 435mg | Fiber: 3g | Carbohydrates: 12g

Jerked Lobster with Coconut

Spicy jerked lobster served with toast points makes an easy and delicious treat. Try serving this with Oven-Roasted Corn in Chili Coconut Milk (see Chapter 15).

INGREDIENTS | SERVES 8

2 tablespoons coconut ghee

8 slices thinly sliced bread

½ cup coconut milk

1 cup unsweetened cream of coconut

2 tablespoons dry jerk seasoning

4 medium-sized lobsters, shelled and cut into chunks

Salt and pepper, to taste

¼ cup freshly grated Parmesan cheese

Lobster

Lobsters, like crabs, are either purchased alive or already cooked, due to the rapid deterioration of their bodies after they die. Eating lobster or crab that was dead before cooking could result in a serious food-borne illness!

1. Preheat the oven to 375° F. Place a wire rack inside a shallow baking sheet.

2. Mix ghee and a dash of salt; spread onto both sides of the bread and cut each slice in half diagonally.

3. Line slices of bread evenly on the wire rack; bake for 8 minutes and turn over. Bake for another 5 minutes, until toast points are crisp and golden brown, but not burned. Remove from oven and set aside.

4. In a large saucepan over medium heat, mix coconut milk and cream of coconut for about 5 minutes.

5. Add dry jerk seasoning, lobster chunks, and salt and pepper, to taste. Reduce to low heat; simmer about 10 minutes.

6. Pour lobster mixture into a 9" × 13" baking dish, sprinkle with Parmesan. Bake for 20 minutes.

7. Remove from oven, and serve over toast points.

PER SERVING Calories: 312 | Fat: 21g | Protein: 18g | Sodium: 410mg | Fiber: 1g | Carbohydrates: 14g

Seafood Pasta with Creamy Coconut Sauce

This creamy seafood pasta dish makes an elegant meal for entertaining. Try it with a side of Roasted Balsamic Brussels Sprouts (see Chapter 15).

INGREDIENTS | SERVES 8

2 tablespoons coconut oil

1 tablespoon anchovy paste

1 large white onion, diced

1 tablespoon thyme

2 tablespoons fresh basil, chopped

1 (14-ounce) can coconut milk

1 pound large shrimp, peeled and deveined

1 pound cod, cubed

1 pound mussels, sorted and cleaned

¼ cup chicken broth

2 teaspoons potato starch flour

Salt and pepper, to taste

24 ounces dry pasta

Coconut Milk Sauces

Some of the most common sauces made with coconut milk are curry sauces, but you can make any kind of white sauce with coconut milk the same way you can with animal milks. For example, you can make a mushroom sauce, a cheese sauce, or a plain white sauce using coconut milk that is very comparable to its animal-milk counterpart. This is a lifesaver for people who have dairy intolerances!

1. Over medium heat, heat coconut oil in a heavy-bottomed saucepan. Add anchovy paste and onion; sauté for 5 minutes, or until onion becomes translucent.

2. Add thyme, basil, coconut milk, and seafood. Cover and bring to a simmer; cook on medium-low for about 10–15 minutes, until mussels open and shrimp turn pink.

3. Whisk together chicken broth and potato starch flour; whisk into seafood mixture. Add salt and pepper; reduce heat to low.

4. Cook pasta according to directions. Discard any unopened mussels before serving. Serve with seafood coconut sauce.

PER SERVING Calories: 635 | Fat: 20g | Protein: 41g | Sodium: 425mg | Fiber: 3g | Carbohydrates: 73g

Scallops in Coconut Basil Sauce

Good fresh scallops are hard to come by unless you live near the ocean, but you can make these yummy scallops in coconut basil sauce just as well with high-quality frozen scallops from your grocer's freezer.

INGREDIENTS | SERVES 6

2 (14-ounce) cans coconut milk

1 tablespoon fresh ginger, grated

Juice from 2 limes

¼ teaspoon red pepper flakes

3 pounds sea scallops

1 tablespoon fish sauce

2 tablespoons fresh basil, chopped

Scallops

If you live near the coast and can get fresh scallops, fresh are the best. However, if you are not in an area where you can get fresh scallops from a reputable seller, frozen scallops will do just fine. Thaw frozen scallops overnight in the refrigerator—do not thaw in the microwave or at room temperature, as microwaving will change the flavor and texture in unpleasant ways, and thawing scallops at room temperature is like a party invitation for a variety of unpleasant bacteria. If you do not have time to wait, you can thaw them by running cold water over them, but use cold water, not hot.

1. In a large skillet, mix coconut milk, ginger, lime juice, and red pepper flakes. Bring to a boil; reduce heat to medium-low.

2. Add scallops; cook, covered, for about 10 minutes, or until scallops are cooked through. Using a slotted spoon, remove from skillet; place in a serving dish. Cover and set aside.

3. Bring coconut milk mixture to a boil; cook on high heat for about 15 minutes, or until liquid is reduced to about 1½ cups. Add fish sauce and basil. Serve over scallops.

PER SERVING Calories: 457 | Fat: 30g | Protein: 40g | Sodium: 609mg | Fiber: 0g | Carbohydrates: 9g

Thai Coconut Chili Clams and Mussels

This flavorful Thai dish makes a beautiful presentation and a delicious meal, especially when paired with Pea Tendrils with Coconut (see Chapter 15).

INGREDIENTS | **SERVES 6**

4 tablespoons coconut oil

1 cup minced shallots

2 tablespoons fresh ginger, grated

3 cloves garlic, minced

2 (14-ounce) cans coconut milk

⅓ cup chili sauce

3 pounds clams, scrubbed and sorted

3 pounds mussels, scrubbed and sorted

4 tablespoons lime juice

½ cup fresh basil leaves, chopped

Sea salt, to taste

2 limes, quartered

¼ cup fresh cilantro, roughly chopped

1. In a large skillet over medium-high heat, heat coconut oil. Add shallots, ginger, and garlic; sauté about 3 minutes, or until shallots are limp. Stir in coconut milk and chili sauce; bring to a boil.

2. Add clams and cover, cooking for about 5 minutes.

3. Add mussels and repeat process, cooking another 5 minutes, or until all shells have opened. Stir in lime juice, basil, and sea salt. Discard any unopened shellfish before serving. Spoon into bowls, and serve with lime wedges and cilantro.

PER SERVING Calories: 485 | Fat: 40g | Protein: 21g | Sodium: 364mg | Fiber: 0g | Carbohydrate: 15g

Clams

When you buy clams, look for clams that are closed. Check for cracked shells. If you see any that are open, tap them gently with one finger and watch to see if they close. If they do not, they are dead and will not be safe to eat.

Fish Roe with Coconut

Fish roe, noted for supporting fertility and stamina, is a traditional food in many cultures. Try this roe pan-fried in coconut oil for energy and vitality!

INGREDIENTS | SERVES 6

1½ cups fish roe
¼ cup water
1 cup fresh grated coconut
3 green chilies, chopped
1 small white onion, chopped
1" piece ginger, grated
½ teaspoon sea salt
2 tablespoons coconut oil

Fish Roe

Fish roe, or fish eggs, are considered a delicacy in many culinary traditions, and are a traditional food known for enhancing fertility in many parts of the world. Roe is used both cooked and raw.

1. In a sieve, thoroughly wash roe and remove membrane. Remove to a cutting board and chop finely.

2. In a medium mixing bowl, place roe. Add water; mix well. Add coconut, green chilies, onion, ginger, and salt.

3. Heat coconut oil in a medium skillet. Add roe mixture; cook over low heat for about 10 minutes, until cooked through.

PER SERVING Calories: 168 | Fat: 12g | Protein: 11g | Sodium: 241mg | Fiber: 2g | Carbohydrates: 6g

CHAPTER 15

Side Dishes

Coconut Rice

Coconut rice is a versatile side dish that complements almost any dish, from stir-fry to curried fish or roasted meats.

INGREDIENTS | SERVES 6

2 cups white rice

1½ cups water

1 (14-ounce) can coconut milk

1 teaspoon sea salt

1. Rinse rice in cold water.

2. In a medium saucepan over high heat, mix rice, water, coconut milk, and salt; bring to a boil. Stir rice; cover with a lid. Reduce heat to low; allow rice to continue cooking for 15 minutes.

3. Remove from the heat; let stand covered for another 10 minutes. Fluff with fork, and serve.

PER SERVING Calories: 354 | Fat: 14g | Protein: 6g | Sodium: 400mg | Fiber: 1g | Carbohydrates: 51g

Creamy Scalloped Potatoes

These potatoes are a delicious complement to almost any vegetable side dish, and can turn any meal from plain to posh.

INGREDIENTS | SERVES 6

5 large red potatoes
2 large onions
¼ cup coconut ghee plus 1 tablespoon
4 cloves garlic, minced
1 teaspoon curry powder
1½ cups coconut milk
2 teaspoons potato starch flour
Sea salt and freshly ground black pepper, to taste

1. Preheat the oven to 400°F.

2. Scrub and thinly slice potatoes, about ⅛" thick.

3. Using a cheese grater, grate onions; mix well into the potato slices. Cover and set aside.

4. In a large skillet, heat ¼ cup ghee. Sauté garlic and curry powder just until heated, about 1 minute.

5. Whisk coconut milk and potato starch flour together; add to the skillet. Add salt and pepper; bring to a boil. Remove from heat.

6. Using remaining tablespoon of ghee, grease a 9" × 13" baking pan. Place the potatoes and onions in the pan; pour the coconut milk mixture over the top, stirring slightly with a fork to coat potatoes.

7. Bake, uncovered, for 1½ hours, or until the potatoes are browned and can easily be pierced with a fork.

PER SERVING Calories: 452 | Fat: 24g | Protein: 8g | Sodium: 28mg | Fiber: 6g | Carbohydrates: 58g

Pea Tendrils with Coconut

This simple yet elegant side dish is a fantastic addition to any delicate fish. This can also be served with rice.

INGREDIENTS | SERVES 6

½ pound pea tendrils

2 tablespoons coconut ghee

½ cup fresh coconut, grated

2 green chilies, seeded and finely chopped

½ cup shallots, minced

½ teaspoon salt

¼ teaspoon turmeric

1. Rinse pea tendrils in a colander; gather into a tight bundle and slice crosswise.

2. In a medium pot on high heat, heat coconut ghee; add pea tendrils, grated coconut, chilies, shallots, salt, and turmeric. Mix well, stirring frequently, for 1 minute. Cover and reduce heat to medium-low. Cook another 3 minutes, or until the pea tendrils have wilted and the shallots are tender.

PER SERVING Calories: 86 | Fat: 3g | Protein: 4g | Sodium: 205g | Fiber: 1g | Carbohydrates: 15g

Asparagus in Coconut Milk

This creamy asparagus is a great complement to any pasta dish and also goes well with Creamy Scalloped Potatoes (see recipe in this chapter).

INGREDIENTS | SERVES 6

1 pound asparagus
1 tablespoon coconut oil
1 teaspoon fresh ginger, grated
1 clove garlic, pressed
1 cup coconut milk
Sea salt, to taste

Asparagus

For the best quality, when choosing asparagus, look for spears with a larger diameter. Tips should be firm and tight, and the stems should be flexible and not woody. Asparagus is best early in the spring.

1. Wash asparagus and cut into 1" pieces.

2. In a saucepan over medium heat, heat coconut oil. Add ginger and garlic; sauté for 1 minute.

3. Add coconut milk and asparagus; simmer for 10–15 minutes, until sauce is reduced to about ¾ cup and asparagus is tender, but not overcooked. Remove from heat, and salt to taste.

PER SERVING Calories: 110 | Fat: 10g | Protein: 2g | Sodium: 7mg | Fiber: 2g | Carbohydrates: 4g

Stir-Fried Coconut Green Beans

These yummy stir-fried green beans make a delicious and attractive side and go well with any meat entrée.

INGREDIENTS | SERVES 6

3 tablespoons coconut oil
2 teaspoons yellow split peas
3 whole dried red chilies
1 teaspoon cumin seeds
¾ pound green beans
1 teaspoon sea salt plus more, to taste
½ cup unsweetened shredded coconut
1 cup water

1. In a wok over high heat, heat coconut oil. Add split peas; stir-fry for 3 minutes, until browned.

2. Add chilies and cumin seeds; cook, stirring frequently, for 1 minute.

3. Trim ends of green beans and cut into 1" pieces. Add green beans and 1 teaspoon salt to the wok; cook for another 5 minutes.

4. Add coconut and water. Cover and bring to a simmer; cook another 10 minutes, or until beans are tender.

5. Uncover and simmer on low heat for another 5 minutes, or until water has evaporated, being careful not to burn. Add salt to taste, and serve.

PER SERVING Calories: 115 | Fat: 9g | Protein: 2g | Sodium: 394mg | Fiber: 4g | Carbohydrates: 8g

Ginger–Sweet Potato Casserole with Coconut Milk

This casserole is a delightful and much healthier alternative to the holiday sweet potatoes with marshmallow topping!

INGREDIENTS | SERVES 8

Coconut oil as needed to grease pan plus 2 tablespoons

1 can coconut milk

⅓ cup raw coconut sugar

1 tablespoon orange zest

½ teaspoon sea salt

3" fresh ginger, grated

½ teaspoon powdered nutmeg

⅛ teaspoon cloves

½ cup fresh coconut, grated, divided

4 cups sweet potatoes, thinly sliced

1. Preheat the oven to 325°F. Grease a 9" × 9" baking pan with coconut oil until well coated.

2. In a small bowl, mix coconut milk, sugar, orange zest, salt, and spices.

3. In a small saucepan, melt 2 tablespoons coconut oil.

4. Mix ¼ cup coconut with sweet potatoes; add to the baking dish. Drizzle with warmed coconut oil, making sure sweet potatoes are well coated. Pour coconut milk mixture over sweet potatoes; stir until well mixed.

5. Bake, uncovered, for 30 minutes. Remove from oven and stir, paying close attention to the edges. Sprinkle with remaining coconut and return to the oven. Bake for another 45 minutes. Remove from oven, and serve.

PER SERVING Calories: 244 | Fat: 16g | Protein: 2g | Sodium: 194mg | Fiber: 3g | Carbohydrates: 26g

Plantains in Coconut Milk

These slightly sweet plantains simmered in coconut milk, lightly seasoned with cinnamon and cloves, make a scrumptious addition to any meal.

INGREDIENTS | SERVES 6

4 plantains, sliced

¼ teaspoon salt

1 teaspoon curry powder

½ teaspoon cinnamon

⅛ teaspoon cloves

2 cups coconut milk

1. In a heavy saucepan, mix plantains, salt, curry, cinnamon, and cloves.

2. Pour coconut milk over plantains and spices. Bring to a simmer over low heat for 10 minutes, or until plantains are tender and milk is absorbed. Serve hot.

PER SERVING Calories: 296 | Fat: 17g | Protein: 3g | Sodium: 112mg | Fiber: 3g | Carbohydrates: 41g

What is the difference between a plantain and a banana?

Bananas and plantains belong to the same family, but bananas are very sweet and moist compared to a plantain. Plantains are traditionally eaten cooked, much like potatoes.

Cabbage with Coconut Vinegar

This steamed cabbage dish is a unique and more flavorful version of the old boiled cabbage staple.

INGREDIENTS | SERVES 6

1 head cabbage, chopped

1 cup water

¼ cup coconut ghee

¼ cup coconut vinegar

3 strips bacon, cooked and crumbled

Sea salt and pepper, to taste

1. In a large skillet, place cabbage; add water and cover. Bring to a boil; reduce heat. Cook, covered, for 10 minutes, or until cabbage is tender.

2. In a saucepan, heat ghee until melted, about 1 minute. Add vinegar and crumbled bacon; mix well.

3. Drain excess water from cabbage. Drizzle with ghee mixture; toss to coat. Add salt and pepper, to taste, and serve while hot.

PER SERVING Calories: 139 | Fat: 11g | Protein: 3g | Sodium: 122mg | Fiber: 4g | Carbohydrates: 9g

Coconut Garlic Mashed Potatoes

Coconut Garlic Mashed Potatoes are a great twist on the traditional plain mashed potatoes.

INGREDIENTS | SERVES 6

6 medium Yukon Gold potatoes, well scrubbed and cubed

6 cloves garlic, peeled

4 cups water

½ cup coconut milk

½ cup Coconut Sour Cream (see Chapter 20)

2 tablespoons coconut ghee

1 teaspoon salt

¼ teaspoon freshly ground black pepper

Potatoes

The peels of the potato are filled with nutrients! However, conventional growing methods contaminate potato peels with chemical fertilizers and pesticides. To get the best nutrition from potatoes, get organically grown potatoes and leave the skins on.

1. In a large saucepan, place potatoes and garlic cloves; cover with water. Cook, covered, on high heat for 5 minutes, or until potatoes come to a boil. Reduce to medium-low heat; simmer for 10 minutes, or until potatoes are soft enough to easily pierce with a fork.

2. Drain potatoes; add coconut milk, Coconut Sour Cream, and ghee.

3. Using a hand mixer, beat potatoes until fluffy. Add salt and pepper; stir until well mixed. Serve hot.

PER SERVING Calories: 249 | Fat: 10g | Protein: 4g | Sodium: 405mg | Fiber: 6g | Carbohydrates: 40g

Oven-Roasted Corn in Chili Coconut Milk

This oven-roasted corn on the cob makes a great side to go with Slow-Cooked Coconut Shredded-Beef Taco Filling (see Chapter 13) and Coconut Black Beans (see recipe in this chapter).

INGREDIENTS | SERVES 6

1 (14-ounce) can coconut milk

2 tablespoons coconut ghee

1 teaspoon chili powder

1 dash red pepper flakes

1 teaspoon sea salt

⅛ teaspoon freshly ground black pepper

6 ears of fresh, husked corn

Cooking in Coconut Milk

Many traditional dishes around the world use coconut milk. Beans, rice, and a variety of meats and vegetables are often simmered in coconut milk.

1. Whisk together coconut milk, coconut ghee, chili powder, red pepper, salt, and pepper. Pour into a greased 9" × 13" baking pan.

2. Add corn; turn to coat with milk mixture. Let marinate in the refrigerator for 3 hours, turning corn every 20 minutes.

3. Preheat the oven to 425°F.

4. Place corn in the oven and bake for 15 minutes. Turn corn and cook another 15 minutes. Serve hot.

PER SERVING Calories: 246 | Fat: 20g | Protein: 4g | Sodium: 414mg | Fiber: 3g | Carbohydrates: 19g

Coconut Garlic Roasted Cowboy Fries

Serve this simple yet tasty side with your favorite ranch dressing.

INGREDIENTS | SERVES 6

6 medium russet potatoes, quartered lengthwise into wedges

2 tablespoons coconut oil

½ teaspoon sea salt

1 teaspoon garlic powder

1. Preheat the oven to 375°F.

2. Spread potato wedges out on a baking sheet.

3. Mix coconut oil with salt and garlic powder. Using a basting brush, coat each potato wedge with a thin layer.

4. Bake for 20–30 minutes, or until potato wedges are golden brown and can be easily pierced with a fork.

PER SERVING Calories: 187 | Fat: 5g | Protein: 4g | Sodium: 207mg | Fiber: 5g | Carbohydrates: 37g

Roasted-Coconut Lemon-Garlic-Ginger Carrots

These lemon ginger carrots with a hint of coconut and garlic are delicious with Coconut Garlic Mashed Potatoes (see recipe in this chapter) and salmon.

INGREDIENTS | SERVES 6

3 tablespoons coconut ghee, melted

3 tablespoons lemon juice

3 cloves garlic, pressed

1" piece fresh ginger, grated

Sea salt and freshly ground black pepper, to taste

3 cups fresh carrots, peeled and sliced

1. Preheat the oven to 400°F

2. Using 1 teaspoon coconut ghee, grease a 9" × 9" baking pan.

3. Whisk together remaining coconut ghee, lemon juice, garlic, and ginger; add salt and pepper, to taste.

4. Add carrots to baking pan; drizzle ghee mixture over all, tossing to coat. Bake for 35 minutes, or until carrots are tender.

PER SERVING Calories: 89 | Fat: 7g | Protein: 1g | Sodium: 43mg | Fiber: 2g | Carbohydrates: 7g

Coconut Cream of Mushroom Green Bean Casserole

This creamy classic green bean casserole is a great dish for potlucks or family gatherings!

INGREDIENTS | **SERVES 6**

2 quarts water plus 1 tablespoon
1½ pounds fresh green beans
1 tablespoon coconut ghee
½ pound portobello mushrooms
3 cloves garlic, minced
Sea salt and pepper, to taste
1 teaspoon potato starch flour
½ cup coconut milk
½ cup chicken broth
½ cup Cheddar cheese, grated (optional)
1 cup French fried onions

1. In a large pot with a steamer insert, bring 2 quarts of water to a boil.

2. Cut beans into 1" pieces; add to steamer insert and cook, covered, for 5 minutes.

3. In a large skillet, heat ghee. Add mushrooms, garlic, salt, and pepper. Sauté until mushrooms are tender, about 2 minutes.

4. In a small bowl, whisk potato starch flour into 1 tablespoon of water; add to the mushrooms. Cook 1 minute, until mixture thickens; whisk in coconut milk and chicken broth. Simmer about 5–10 minutes, then stir in the beans.

5. Preheat the oven to 425°F.

6. Pour the green bean mixture into a casserole dish. If you are using cheese, sprinkle top of casserole with grated Cheddar and top with French fried onions. Bake for about 15 minutes, or until bubbly. Allow to cool for 5–10 minutes before serving.

PER SERVING Calories: 210 | Fat: 15g | Protein: 4g | Sodium: 347mg | Fiber: 5g | Carbohydrates: 17g

Coconut Black Beans

Bring a little Caribbean to your house for dinner tonight with these delicious black beans cooked in coconut milk.

INGREDIENTS | SERVES 6

2 cups dried black beans
4 cups water
2 tablespoons coconut oil
3 large cloves garlic, pressed
1 small white onion, chopped
2 whole dried chilies
1 tablespoon cumin
1 (14-ounce) can coconut milk
Sea salt and pepper, to taste

Cooking Beans

When cooking dried beans, remember that every 1 cup of dried beans is equal to 3 cups of beans soaked and cooked.

1. Rinse and drain beans.

2. In a medium saucepan, mix beans and water; bring to a boil and reduce heat. Allow to simmer on medium-low heat for 45 minutes.

3. While beans are simmering, in a medium saucepan over medium heat, heat coconut oil. Add garlic and onion; sauté for about 5 minutes, or until onion is translucent. Add chili peppers, cumin, and coconut milk.

4. Remove beans from heat; drain and rinse. Add to coconut milk mixture; add salt and pepper, to taste. Simmer for another 15 minutes, or until done. Remove from heat, and serve.

PER SERVING Calories: 399 | Fat: 20g | Protein: 16g | Sodium: 14mg | Fiber: 10g | Carbohydrate: 44g

Roasted Balsamic Brussels Sprouts

Coconut oil and balsamic vinegar add a little zing to Brussels sprouts. Try adding Coconut Garlic Mashed Potatoes (see recipe in this chapter) and serving with chicken or fish.

INGREDIENTS | SERVES 6

1 pound Brussels sprouts

2 tablespoons coconut oil plus more as needed

2 tablespoons balsamic vinegar

Sea salt and pepper, to taste

1. Preheat the oven to 375°F.

2. Peel off the tough outer layer of Brussels sprouts and slice each one in half.

3. Melt 2 tablespoons coconut oil; mix with vinegar. Using a basting brush, coat Brussels sprouts evenly; salt and pepper, to taste.

4. Using additional coconut oil, grease a baking sheet. Place Brussels sprouts on the baking sheet; roast in the oven for about 10 minutes. Turn and roast for another 10 minutes, or until lightly browned and easily pierced with a fork. Remove from oven, and serve.

PER SERVING Calories: 76 | Fat: 5g | Protein: 3g | Sodium: 20mg | Fiber: 3g | Carbohydrates: 8g

Vegetable Medley with Coconut-Vinegar Butter Sauce

This steamed vegetable medley drizzled in coconut-vinegar butter sauce is delicious with chicken or fish.

INGREDIENTS | SERVES 6

1 large handful snow peas
¼ cup coconut ghee
2 tablespoons coconut vinegar
Sea salt, to taste
1 large head cauliflower
4 large carrots, peeled and sliced

Cooking Vegetables

For best results, steam vegetables until tender-crisp. This gives you the freshest flavor and the most nutrition. Goitrogen vegetables like cauliflower, broccoli, cabbage, kale, and spinach should always be lightly steamed before eating, or avoided if you have a slow thyroid.

1. Rinse snow peas and remove any tough ends, pulling out the string that runs down the side.

2. In a small saucepan over medium heat, mix ghee, vinegar, and salt, to taste, until ghee is melted and mixture is well combined. Set aside.

3. Cut cauliflower into large chunks. Mix cauliflower and carrots in a steamer; cook over high heat for about 5 minutes.

4. Add snow peas; cook another 5 minutes, or until cooked through, but slightly crisp. Remove from heat, and drizzle with coconut-vinegar butter sauce.

PER SERVING Calories: 141 | Fat: 9g | Protein: 4g | Sodium: 76mg | Fiber: 5g | Carbohydrates: 13g

Coconut Green Curry Rice

This curry rice makes a great side for raw marinated fish.

INGREDIENTS | SERVES 6

3 cups uncooked rice

2 tablespoons whey

7½ cups water

½ cup coconut oil

1 large onion, chopped

4 cloves garlic, pressed

4 tablespoons green curry paste

3 vegetarian bouillon cubes

1½ cups coconut milk

1 bunch parsley, chopped

4 zucchinis, chopped

3 bell peppers, diced

1 cup raw cashews, chopped

Raw Coconut Oil

If you want to make sure that your coconut oil is extra virgin and raw, you will want to get cold-processed coconut oil that has not been heated. Expeller pressing uses a corkscrew press, and while the process itself doesn't use heat, the high pressure from the oil press does heat the oil quite a bit.

1. In a large mixing bowl, mix rice, whey, and 6 cups water; allow to soak overnight, up to 24 hours.

2. In a large pot over low heat, melt coconut oil; add onion and garlic, and warm for 20 minutes.

3. Stir in green curry paste, 1½ cups of water, bouillon cubes, coconut milk, parsley, zucchini, bell pepper, and cashews.

4. Drain rice; add to sauce. Mix well, and serve.

PER SERVING Calories: 795 | Fat: 41g | Protein: 15g | Sodium: 63mg | Fiber: 7g | Carbohydrates: 97g

CHAPTER 16

Soups and Salads

Carrot Ginger Coconut Soup

*This hot Carrot Ginger Coconut Soup is a great way to warm your bones
on a cold winter night. Grab a bowl and cozy up by the fire!*

INGREDIENTS | SERVES 6

6 cups chicken broth
1 teaspoon coconut oil
1 small onion, chopped
1 garlic clove, pressed
1 teaspoon fresh ginger, grated
1 medium red potato, peeled and cubed
6 carrots, peeled and chopped
1 cup coconut milk
½ teaspoon pepper

1. In a large heavy-bottomed saucepan, heat broth on medium-high for about 10 minutes, or until broth is reduced by half.

2. In a medium skillet over medium heat, heat oil. Add onion and garlic; sauté for 5 minutes, or until onion is translucent.

3. Add ginger, potato, and carrots to the broth; cover and bring to a boil. Reduce heat; simmer another 5 minutes.

4. Add coconut milk, pepper, onions, and garlic; continue to simmer for another 5 minutes, or until potato and carrot pieces can be easily pierced with a fork.

5. Carefully add soup to a food processor, in batches if necessary, and purée until smooth. Serve hot.

PER SERVING Calories: 168 | Fat: 9g | Protein: 7g | Sodium: 758mg | Fiber: 4g | Carbohydrates: 16g

Coconut Butternut Squash Chowder

This savory butternut chowder is deliciously filling, and goes well with a piece of crusty bread and butter.

INGREDIENTS | SERVES 6

1 medium butternut squash
1 tablespoon coconut ghee, melted
4 bacon slices, cut into ½" pieces
1 yellow onion, chopped
2 celery stalks, chopped
1 bay leaf
1 teaspoon fresh sage, chopped, plus a few small sage leaves for garnish
4 teaspoons sea salt
1 teaspoon pepper
2 medium russet potatoes, peeled and cubed
3 cups chicken broth
½ cup coconut cream

1. Preheat the oven to 375°F.

2. Cut squash lengthwise with a sharp knife; remove and discard seeds. Place on a large baking sheet and brush with melted ghee. Bake for 45 minutes, flesh side up, until squash is cooked through. Remove from oven, and cool.

3. In a large skillet, cook bacon over medium heat for about 5 minutes, or until crispy. Using tongs, transfer bacon to a paper-towel-lined plate. Set aside.

4. Pour off all but about 1 tablespoon of bacon fat; return the skillet to medium heat. Add onion, celery, bay leaf, chopped sage, salt, and pepper; sauté for 5 minutes, or until onions are translucent.

5. Add potatoes; cover and cook an additional 5 minutes, stirring occasionally.

6. Add broth; simmer, stirring to scrape up the browned bits, for about 2 minutes. Bring to a boil and reduce heat to low; simmer for another 10–15 minutes, or until potatoes are soft.

7. Scoop squash out of skins and put into a food processor; purée until smooth. Add to the broth mixture along with crumbled bacon; simmer for another 5 minutes.

8. Stir in the coconut cream; add additional salt and pepper, to taste. Remove the bay leaf and discard. Scoop chowder into soup bowls and garnish with sage leaves. Serve hot.

PER SERVING Calories: 177 | Fat: 12g | Protein: 5g | Sodium: 1869mg | Fiber: 3g | Carbohydrates: 16g

Plantain and Coconut Beef Stew

Try this delicious Caribbean twist on an all-American comfort food with warm crusty bread!

INGREDIENTS | SERVES 6

1 cup coconut water
2 pounds stew beef
Salt and pepper, to taste
2 tablespoons coconut oil
2 large white onions, finely chopped
1 large ripe tomato, peeled and chopped
1½ cups coconut milk
5 unripe plantains

1. In a medium pot, heat coconut water on high. Add stew beef, salt, and pepper; cover and cook, stirring occasionally, for about 10 minutes, or until meat is tender. Set aside.

2. In a large skillet, heat coconut oil; add onions. Sauté for about 5 minutes, or until onions are translucent.

3. Add tomato and meat; continue cooking until tomatoes soften, about 5 minutes.

4. Add the coconut milk, stirring constantly; bring to a boil and reduce heat.

5. Peel and cut plantains into large pieces; add to the stew. Continue simmering for 10–15 minutes, or until plantains are cooked but firm. Serve hot.

PER SERVING Calories: 740 | Fat: 47g | Protein: 30g | Sodium: 162mg | Fiber: 5g | Carbohydrates: 56g

Coconut Lamb Stew

This savory lamb stew makes a satisfying meal on a cold day.

INGREDIENTS | SERVES 6

3 tablespoons coconut oil

3 sweet neem leaves

1 teaspoon ground cinnamon

1 teaspoon ground cardamom

½ teaspoon ground cloves

½ teaspoon black pepper

1 medium onion, chopped

2 pounds boneless lamb, cut into 1" pieces

1 (14-ounce) can coconut milk

2 large russet potatoes, peeled and cubed

4 medium carrots, peeled and sliced

¼ teaspoon ground turmeric

1 tablespoon ground coriander

⅛ teaspoon cayenne pepper

2 teaspoons sea salt

1. In a large skillet, heat coconut oil; add neem leaves, cinnamon, cardamom, cloves, and pepper. Stir together; add onion. Sauté for 3 minutes, or until onion is soft.

2. Add meat; cook over medium-low heat, stirring occasionally, for 5 minutes, or until meat is browned.

3. Add coconut milk; cook for 1 minute. Stir, scraping the bottom to loosen brown bits; transfer to a large soup pot and add potatoes, carrots, turmeric, coriander, cayenne, and salt.

4. Cover and bring to a boil; reduce heat and simmer for about 1 hour, or until meat and potatoes are tender. Serve hot.

PER SERVING Calories: 513 | Fat: 30g | Protein: 35g | Sodium: 922mg | Fiber: 5g | Carbohydrates: 29g

Spicy Sweet Potato and Coconut Soup

A little spicy and a little sweet! This exotic soup is surprisingly easy to make.

INGREDIENTS | SERVES 6

2 pounds sweet potatoes
1 tablespoon coconut oil
1 medium onion, chopped
2" piece fresh gingerroot, grated
1 tablespoon red curry paste
1 (14-ounce) can coconut milk
3 cups chicken broth
3½ tablespoons lemon juice
1 teaspoon sea salt
½ cup fresh cilantro, chopped

1. Preheat the oven to 400°F.

2. Pierce sweet potatoes several times with a fork; place directly onto the oven rack. Place a foil-lined baking sheet on the bottom rack to catch drips; bake 45 minutes, or until potatoes can easily be pierced with a fork. Remove from the oven, and cool.

3. In a large soup pot, heat coconut oil over medium heat. Add onion and ginger; sauté 5 minutes, or until onion is translucent.

4. Add curry paste; sauté another minute, then whisk in coconut milk and broth. Bring to a boil; reduce to low heat and simmer for another 5 minutes.

5. Peel sweet potatoes and cut into 1" cubes. Add to the soup pot; cook, covered, for 5 more minutes.

6. Add lemon juice, salt, and cilantro; stir to mix. Serve hot.

PER SERVING Calories: 300 | Fat: 17g | Protein: 5g | Sodium: 658mg | Fiber: 6g | Carbohydrates: 36g

Vietnamese Clam Chowder

Lemongrass gives this tasty Vietnamese chowder a bit of zing!

INGREDIENTS | SERVES 6

1 teaspoon coconut ghee

3 medium russet potatoes, peeled and cubed

1 large onion, chopped

½ cup celery, including leaves, chopped

1 tablespoon fresh ginger, grated

2 garlic cloves, pressed

1 fresh lemongrass stalk, peeled and crushed

1½ tablespoons fish sauce

1 medium zucchini, chopped

2 (6.5-ounce) cans chopped clams, drained

⅔ cup coconut milk

Juice of 2 limes

2 tablespoons fresh cilantro, chopped

1. In a large skillet over medium heat, melt ghee. Add potatoes, onion, celery, ginger, and garlic; sauté 5 minutes, or until celery and onion are tender.

2. Stir in lemongrass and fish sauce. Bring to a boil; reduce heat and simmer, uncovered, for 10–15 minutes, or until potatoes are tender.

3. Add zucchini and clams. Return to a boil; reduce heat to medium-low and simmer another 5 minutes.

4. Stir in coconut milk, lime juice, and cilantro; remove from heat. Remove and discard crushed lemongrass stalk before serving.

PER SERVING Calories: 244 | Fat: 8g | Protein: 19g | Sodium: 437mg | Fiber: 4g | Carbohydrates: 28g

Strawberry Soup with Grated Coconut

This yummy dessert soup will top off any meal with flair!

INGREDIENTS | SERVES 8

2 pounds fresh strawberries
2 tablespoons raw honey
3 cups coconut milk yogurt
1 cup coconut cream
6 tablespoons grated coconut

1. Wash, hull, and halve strawberries.

2. In food processor, purée berries and honey until smooth.

3. Pour strawberry mixture through a fine sieve to remove seeds.

4. Return to processor; add yogurt and cream. Blend only until mixed.

5. Chill for 15 minutes; pour into bowls, and serve cold with grated coconut sprinkled on top.

PER SERVING Calories: 262 | Fat: 19g | Protein: 3g | Sodium: 10mg | Fiber: 6g | Carbohydrates: 25g

Coconut Curry Corn Soup

This sweet and spicy corn soup makes an easy and impressive dish.

INGREDIENTS | SERVES 6

1 tablespoon coconut oil

2 large onions, finely chopped

1 tablespoon red curry paste

1 (14-ounce) can coconut milk

4 cups frozen kernel corn, thawed

2 cups water

½ teaspoon sea salt

1. In a large skillet, heat oil over medium heat. Add onions; sauté for 5 minutes, or until softened. Add curry paste and coconut milk.

2. Transfer to slow cooker; add corn, water, and salt. Cover and cook on low heat for 6 hours.

3. Using an immersion blender, carefully blend soup until smooth. Serve hot.

PER SERVING Calories: 251 | Fat: 17g | Protein: 5g | Sodium: 208mg | Fiber: 3g | Carbohydrates: 26g

Fruit Salad with Coconut Dressing

This yummy tropical fruit salad makes a quick dessert.

INGREDIENTS | **SERVES 6**

2 oranges
1 pineapple
2 kiwi fruit
1 apple
1 banana
¾ cup coconut milk
1 tablespoon raw honey
Juice of 1 lemon
Seeds from 1 pomegranate
1 tablespoon fresh mint, chopped

1. Peel, core, and cut fruit; mix in a large bowl.

2. Add coconut milk, honey, and lemon; mix well.

3. Top with pomegranate seeds and mint before serving.

PER SERVING Calories: 257 | Fat: 7g | Protein: 3g | Sodium: 8mg | Fiber: 5g | Carbohydrates: 52g

Sweet Potato Coconut Salad

This sweet potato salad makes a nice alternative to baked yams.

INGREDIENTS | SERVES 6

6 medium sweet potatoes, scrubbed
Water, as needed
½ cup coconut sugar
1 cup shredded coconut
½ cup pecans, finely chopped
½ cup currants
¼ cup coconut ghee

1. In a large pot, add sweet potatoes and enough water to cover potatoes by 2"; bring to a boil over medium-high heat.

2. Reduce heat to medium-low; simmer for about 40 minutes, or until potatoes are just tender and can be easily pierced with a fork.

3. Remove the potatoes from heat and drain water. When potatoes are cooled enough to handle, peel and cut into 1" pieces.

4. In a large bowl, combine potatoes, sugar, coconut, pecans, currants, and ghee. With a potato masher, mash ingredients together until well mixed but still lumpy. Chill overnight before serving.

PER SERVING Calories: 439 | Fat: 24g | Protein: 4g | Sodium: 77mg | Fiber: 8g | Carbohydrates: 56g

Toasted Coconut Green Salad

This tasty sweet and savory green salad with raspberry vinaigrette dressing makes a great side.

INGREDIENTS | SERVES 6

1 small head red leaf lettuce

1 small head romaine lettuce

1 cup fresh baby spinach greens

2 slices bacon, cooked crisp and crumbled

½ cup sliced strawberries

½ cup fresh grated coconut, toasted

½ cup raw almonds, slivered

¼ cup coconut oil, melted

¼ cup olive oil

½ cup coconut vinegar

1 tablespoon raspberries, mashed

1. Rinse greens. In a large mixing bowl, tear lettuce into bite-sized pieces and add spinach; toss until evenly mixed.

2. Add bacon, strawberries, coconut, and almonds. Mix well and set aside.

3. In a blender, combine melted coconut oil and olive oil; mix well.

4. Add coconut vinegar and raspberries; blend until smooth.

5. Pour into a serving container, and serve with dressing on the side.

PER SERVING Calories: 286 | Fat: 26g | Protein: 5g | Sodium: 89mg | Fiber: 5g | Carbohydrates: 10g

Mango Coconut Salad

This yummy mango coconut rice salad doubles as a side dish and a dessert!

INGREDIENTS | SERVES 6

1 teaspoon coconut ghee

½ cup uncooked basmati rice

Sea salt, to taste

2 cups water

2 tablespoons fresh basil, chopped

½ cup camargue red rice

1 red bell pepper, cored and thinly sliced

1 tablespoon fresh mint leaves, roughly chopped

1 tablespoon cilantro, roughly chopped

1 small white onion, thinly sliced

1 large mango, seeded and cubed

¼ cup roasted salted peanuts, roughly chopped

2 tablespoons coconut oil, melted

¼ cup flaked coconut

1. In a small saucepan, heat ghee over medium heat; add basmati rice and salt. Sauté for 3 minutes; add 1 cup of water and 1 tablespoon basil. Cover and bring to a boil; reduce heat to medium-low. Simmer for about 20 minutes. Remove from heat, and allow rice to cool.

2. Rinse saucepan; add red rice and remaining water. Cover and bring to a boil. Reduce heat and simmer for 20 minutes, or until cooked through. Remove from heat, and cool.

3. In a large bowl, mix cooled rice, remaining basil, bell pepper, mint, cilantro, onion, mango, peanuts, coconut oil, and coconut. Toss to mix well, and serve.

PER SERVING Calories: 226 | Fat: 9g | Protein: 5g | Sodium: 23mg | Fiber: 3g | Carbohydrates: 34g

Coconut Ginger Salad

This sweet coconut ginger salad with green apples makes a nice tangy side for a hot day.

INGREDIENTS | SERVES 6

2 stalks fresh lemongrass, tender inner white bulbs only, crushed

½ cup coconut oil, melted

Sea salt and freshly ground black pepper, to taste

6 Granny Smith apples, cored, quartered, and cubed

½ small yellow onion, thinly sliced

3" piece ginger, peeled and cut into ⅛" × 2" matchsticks

½ cup fresh coconut, finely grated

3 tablespoons fresh lemon juice

2 tablespoons basil, finely chopped

1. In a blender, add lemongrass and coconut oil. Blend until just combined. Pour oil into a jar and let stand for 1 hour in a warm place; strain, pressing solids to extract as much oil as possible. Add salt to taste.

2. In a large bowl, add apples, onion, ginger, coconut, lemon juice, and basil; add salt and pepper, to taste.

3. Add lemongrass oil; toss together until well coated. Serve.

PER SERVING Calories: 286 | Fat: 21g | Protein: 1g | Sodium: 4mg | Fiber: 5g | Carbohydrates: 29g

Coconut-Cashew Rice Salad

This savory rice salad makes a great side dish.

INGREDIENTS | SERVES 6

4 tablespoons coconut oil, divided use

1 medium yellow onion, halved and thinly sliced

1 clove garlic, pressed

1 tablespoon fresh ginger, grated

2 cups uncooked basmati rice

Sea salt and freshly ground black pepper, to taste

¼ cup raw cashews, halved

2 cups coconut milk

2 cups water

½ cup green onion, thinly sliced

¼ cup grated fresh coconut

1. In a large skillet, heat 3 tablespoons coconut oil over medium heat. Add onion, garlic, and ginger; sauté until soft, about 5 minutes.

2. In a colander, rinse rice; add to the skillet. Add salt and pepper, to taste; sauté for another 3 minutes, or until rice begins to brown.

3. In a small skillet, heat remaining coconut oil; add cashews and sauté for 3 minutes, or until lightly browned. Drain on paper towels.

4. In a medium saucepan over medium heat, mix coconut milk and water and bring to a simmer. Add rice mixture; bring to a boil. Cover and reduce heat to medium-low; simmer for 20 minutes, and remove from heat.

5. Stir in green onion and coconut. Serve topped with cashews.

PER SERVING Calories: 505 | Fat: 29g | Protein: 7g | Sodium: 16mg | Fiber: 2g | Carbohydrates: 56g

Carrot Coconut Salad

This tangy carrot salad with dried currants and slivered almonds makes a nice summer snack.

INGREDIENTS | SERVES 6

3 cups grated carrots

½ cup grated coconut

¼ cup currants

¼ cup slivered almonds

1 tablespoon olive oil

2 tablespoons coconut oil, melted

2 tablespoons coconut vinegar

1 tablespoon coconut sugar

¼ teaspoon sea salt

1. Toss together carrots, coconut, currants, and almonds until well mixed.

2. Mix oils, vinegar, and sugar. Pour over carrot mixture; stir to coat. Add salt, and serve.

PER SERVING Calories: 131 | Fat: 9g | Protein: 1g | Sodium: 137mg | Fiber: 3g | Carbohydrates: 13g

CHAPTER 17

Breads and Desserts

Gluten-Free Coconut Pizza Dough

Try this tasty gluten-free herbed pizza crust with your choice of toppings.

INGREDIENTS | SERVES 6

3 eggs

1 cup coconut milk

1 clove garlic, pressed

½ cup coconut flour

¼ cup flax meal

½ teaspoon baking powder

½ teaspoon sea salt

1 teaspoon dried oregano

1 teaspoon dried basil

½ cup rice flour

¼ cup potato starch flour

1. Preheat the oven to 375°F.

2. In a medium bowl, beat together eggs and coconut milk; add garlic, coconut flour, flax meal, baking powder, salt, oregano, and basil.

3. Stir together rice flour and potato starch flour until well mixed. Add to dough a little at a time while mixing. Mix well.

4. Pat dough into a parchment-lined cookie sheet, about ½" thick.

5. Bake for 15–20 minutes, or until edges begin to brown. To make a pizza, add toppings of your choice and bake another 5–10 minutes, until heated through and sauce is bubbling. Remove from oven, and cool for 5 minutes before serving.

PER SERVING Calories: 246 | Fat: 13g | Protein: 7g | Sodium: 274mg | Fiber: 6g | Carbohydrates: 27g

Baking Powder Biscuits

These fluffy baking powder biscuits are wonderful hot with butter, and go well with any meal!

INGREDIENTS | SERVES 6

½ cup coconut flour
1 cup rice flour
¼ cup potato starch flour
2 tablespoons baking powder
1 teaspoon sea salt
⅓ cup coconut oil, chilled
1 cup coconut milk

1. Preheat the oven to 400°F. Grease a baking sheet with coconut oil; set aside.

2. In a mixing bowl, combine coconut, rice, and potato starch flours until well mixed.

3. Add baking powder and salt; mix well.

4. Add coconut oil. Using a fork, mix chilled coconut oil into the flour mixture until well mixed and a dry, grainy dough forms.

5. Mix in coconut milk a little at a time, until you have a sticky dough.

6. Using a tablespoon, scoop dough onto greased baking sheet in approximately 1½" balls, about 1" apart. Bake for 10–15 minutes, or until the tops are lightly browned.

PER SERVING Calories: 344 | Fat: 22g | Protein: 4g | Sodium: 869mg | Fiber: 5g | Carbohydrates: 37g

Pani PoPo (Samoan Coconut Rolls)

*These warm rolls, with their gooey coconut sauce topping, will make you
think you have truly died and gone to an island paradise!*

INGREDIENTS | MAKES 12

⅓ cup ground flaxseeds
⅓ cup almond meal
½ cup coconut flour
1½ cups vital wheat gluten
½ cup coconut milk
½ cup yogurt
2 eggs
2 tablespoons coconut oil, melted
2 tablespoons honey
1 teaspoon salt
1 tablespoon active dry yeast
2 (14-ounce) cans coconut cream
2 cups raw coconut sugar

1. Grease a 9" × 13" baking pan with coconut oil.

2. Mix flaxseeds, almond meal, coconut flour, and wheat gluten until well mixed. In a high-powered bread mixer, beat coconut milk, yogurt, eggs, coconut oil, honey, salt, and yeast for 3 minutes. Gradually add in dry ingredients, then knead dough for 3–5 minutes. Set aside.

3. In a medium mixing bowl, mix coconut cream and sugar.

4. Form dough into twelve 1½" balls; place in rows in the greased baking pan. Cover and let rise for 30 minutes, or until rolls have doubled.

5. Preheat the oven to 350°F.

6. Pour coconut cream mixture over uncooked rolls; bake for 45 minutes to 1 hour, or until golden brown. Remove from oven, and let cool slightly before serving.

PER 1 ROLL | Calories: 543 | Fat: 19g | Protein: 16g |
Sodium: 241mg | Fiber: 4g | Carbohydrates: 80g

Coconut Flour Tortillas/Crepes

These coconut flour tortillas are great for wraps or tacos, and can also be used to make a variety of crepes.

INGREDIENTS | SERVES 6

¾ cup coconut flour
6 eggs
½ cup coconut oil
½ teaspoon baking powder
¼ teaspoon sea salt
⅔ cup coconut milk

1. In a food processor, mix flour, eggs, coconut oil, baking powder, and salt until a thick batter forms.

2. Add coconut milk; mix well.

3. Pour batter ¼ cup at a time on a hot tortilla press. Cook for 30 seconds, then open press and flip tortilla; cook for an additional 15 seconds. Repeat process for remaining batter.

PER SERVING Calories: 290 | Fat: 27g | Protein: 5g | Sodium: 163mg | Fiber: 6g | Carbohydrates: 11g

Coconut Quick Bread

This high-protein quick bread makes a great afternoon snack.

INGREDIENTS | SERVES 6

1 cup coconut flour
½ cup coconut ghee
6 eggs
4 tablespoons raw honey
½ teaspoon sea salt
½ teaspoon cinnamon

1. Preheat the oven to 350°F.

2. In a bowl, mix all ingredients together until well combined.

3. Using coconut oil, grease a loaf pan; pour in batter.

4. Bake about 35 minutes, or until golden brown. To test doneness, poke with a toothpick. If the toothpick comes out clean, the bread is done.

PER SERVING Calories: 351 | Fat: 25g | Protein: 9g | Sodium: 264mg | Fiber: 8g | Carbohydrates: 25g

Jamaican Coconut Corn Bread

This Jamaican corn bread goes well with Coconut Black Beans and Coconut Rice (see Chapter 15).

INGREDIENTS | SERVES 6

2 cups yellow cornmeal
½ cup coconut sugar
¼ cup coconut flour
1 teaspoon fresh ginger, grated
1 teaspoon sea salt
1½ teaspoons baking soda
3 eggs
2 tablespoons coconut ghee, melted
¾ cup grated coconut
2 cups coconut milk

1. Preheat the oven to 375°F.

2. In a mixing bowl, combine cornmeal, coconut sugar, and flour.

3. Add ginger, salt, and baking soda; mix well.

4. Add eggs, ghee, ½ cup coconut, and coconut milk; stir until just combined.

5. Grease a 9" × 9" baking pan with coconut oil; add batter. Sprinkle remaining coconut over the top; bake until edges begin to brown, about 18–20 minutes.

PER SERVING Calories: 539 | Fat: 28g | Protein: 10g | Sodium: 746mg | Fiber: 5g | Carbohydrates: 66g

Gluten-Free Sandwich Bread

Try this high-protein gluten-free yeast bread next time you're building a sandwich—you'll be delightfully surprised at its hearty flavor!

INGREDIENTS | SERVES 6

1 tablespoon dry yeast
1 tablespoon coconut sugar
1½ cups warm water
1 cup rice flour
¾ cup sorghum flour
½ cup potato starch flour
¼ cup coconut flour
2 teaspoons xanthan gum
1teaspoon sea salt
3 eggs
1½ tablespoons coconut oil, melted
1 teaspoon coconut water vinegar

1. In a small bowl, mix yeast and sugar. Add warm water; stir together. Set aside.

2. In a large bowl, mix rice, sorghum, potato starch, and coconut flours until well combined. Add xanthan gum and salt; stir well.

3. In a third bowl, whisk the eggs, coconut oil, and vinegar until the eggs are a bit frothy. Add yeast mixture; then mix into the flour mixture.

4. Using a mixer, blending dough for 4–5 minutes.

5. Scoop dough into a well-greased loaf pan. Let rise in warm location until dough is about 1" from the top of the loaf pan, about 20 minutes.

6. Preheat the oven to 375°F.

7. Bake for 1 hour. When bread is done, remove from the oven; let cool before slicing.

PER SERVING Calories: 282 | Fat: 7g | Protein: 7g | Sodium: 425mg | Fiber: 5g | Carbohydrates: 48g

Cheesy Garlic Biscuits

These Cheesy Garlic Biscuits are great with Coconut Lamb Stew (see Chapter 16).

INGREDIENTS | SERVES 6

½ cup coconut flour
1 cup rice flour
¼ cup potato starch flour
2 tablespoons baking powder
1 teaspoon sea salt
2 teaspoons garlic powder
⅓ cup coconut oil, chilled
1 cup coconut milk
⅔ cup Cheddar cheese, grated

1. Preheat the oven to 400°F.

2. Grease a baking sheet with coconut oil. Set aside.

3. In a mixing bowl, combine coconut, rice, and potato starch flours together until well mixed.

4. Add baking powder, salt, and garlic powder; mix well.

5. Add coconut oil. Using a fork, mix chilled coconut oil into the flour mixture until well mixed and a dry, grainy dough forms.

6. Mix in coconut milk a little at a time, until you have a sticky dough; stir in cheese.

7. Using a tablespoon, scoop dough onto greased baking sheet in approximately 1½" balls, about 1" apart. Bake for 10–15 minutes, or until the tops are lightly browned.

PER SERVING Calories: 398 | Fat: 26g | Protein: 7g | Sodium: 948mg | Fiber: 5g | Carbohydrates: 38g

Coconut Cranberry Nut Bread

This coconut cranberry quick bread makes a great Christmas gift.

INGREDIENTS | SERVES 6

8 eggs
½ cup coconut oil, melted
½ cup coconut milk
½ cup raw coconut sugar
1 teaspoon vanilla
½ teaspoon sea salt
⅔ cup sifted coconut flour
1 teaspoon baking powder
1 cup dried cranberries
½ cup pecans, chopped

Coconut Oil and Weight Management

You may expect that coconut oil would cause weight gain because it is a saturated fat. Interestingly, the opposite is true. Coconut has a stabilizing effect on blood sugar, and cannot be stored directly as fat on the body due to its unique structure.

1. Preheat the oven to 350°F.

2. In a large mixing bowl, combine eggs, oil, coconut milk, sugar, vanilla, and salt.

3. Sift together coconut flour and baking powder.

4. Combine wet and dry ingredients; stir in dried cranberries and pecans.

5. Pour batter into a well-greased 9" loaf pan; bake for 1 hour.

PER SERVING Calories: 550 | Fat: 34g | Protein: 13g | Sodium: 367mg | Fiber: 13g | Carbohydrates: 53g

Coconut Teff Pita Bread

Make pocket sandwiches or serve warm with Chicken Vindaloo (see Chapter 13).

INGREDIENTS | SERVES 8

⅔ cup cultured coconut milk
½ cup coconut flour
½ cup dark teff flour
¼ cup potato starch flour
¼ cup brown rice flour
1 small ripe banana
2 teaspoons fresh yeast
2 teaspoons xanthan gum
1 teaspoon sea salt
¼ cup melted coconut oil
1 large egg

1. In a large mixing bowl, combine coconut milk and flours. Cover; let stand overnight.

2. Mash the banana; add it to the flour mixture.

3. Add yeast, xanthan gum, and salt; mix well, and set aside for 1 hour.

4. Mix in coconut oil and egg.

5. On a floured surface, pinch off 2" balls of dough. With a rolling pin, flatten each ball of dough into a 4"–5" round, adding enough additional flour to prevent sticking.

6. Gently place each round on a greased baking sheet; cover for 20 minutes.

7. Preheat the oven to 375°F; place a 9" × 13" baking pan with about 1" of water on the bottom rack of the oven.

8. Sprinkle pitas with water; bake for about 10 minutes, or until they are puffed. Cool on a rack. When pitas are cooled, you can cut them in half and split them for sandwiches or use them to make pita chips.

PER SERVING Calories: 195 | Fat: 9g | Protein: 4g | Sodium: 304mg | Fiber: 6g | Carbohydrates: 25g

Coconut Macaroons

Coconut macaroons are a classic favorite.

INGREDIENTS | MAKES 2 DOZEN

4 large egg whites

¼ teaspoon sea salt

1 cup coconut sugar

1 teaspoon pure almond extract

¼ cup coconut flour

3 cups coconut, freshly grated

1 cup dark chocolate baking chips

1 tablespoon coconut oil

1. Preheat the oven to 375°F.

2. In a medium saucepan over low heat, whisk egg whites, salt, and coconut sugar until dissolved, being careful not to cook egg whites, about 1 minute.

3. Remove from heat; stir in almond extract, coconut flour, and grated coconut. Cover and chill for 1 hour in the refrigerator.

4. Using a tablespoon, drop coconut mixture by spoonfuls onto a parchment-lined baking sheet; bake for 15–20 minutes, or until golden brown. Cool completely, and remove from baking sheet. Replace parchment with a fresh sheet, and set aside.

5. In a double boiler over medium-low heat, melt baking chips with coconut oil; mix well.

6. Dip each coconut macaroon halfway into the melted chocolate, one at a time. Return macaroons to the parchment-lined baking sheet; chill until chocolate is set.

PER SERVING Calories: 136 | Fat: 7g | Protein: 2g | Sodium: 35mg | Fiber: 2g | Carbohydrates: 17g

Chocolate Coconut Cake

This healthier alternative to chocolate cake makes a nice treat for birthdays!

INGREDIENTS | SERVES 8

½ cup coconut oil
1 cup cocoa powder, divided
¼ cup coconut milk
9 eggs
3½ cups coconut sugar, divided
¾ teaspoon sea salt
2 tablespoons vanilla, divided
¾ cup coconut flour, sifted
¾ teaspoon baking powder
2 tablespoons tapioca starch
¼ cup coconut ghee
¼ cup coconut cream

1. Preheat the oven to 350°F.

2. Melt coconut oil in a saucepan over medium heat; add ½ cup cocoa powder and coconut milk. Mix well; remove from heat and set aside.

3. In a mixing bowl, combine eggs, 1½ cups sugar, salt, and 1 tablespoon of vanilla; add to cocoa mixture.

4. Mix coconut flour and baking powder; whisk into batter, mixing until smooth.

5. Pour batter into greased 8" round cake pan; bake for 30 minutes, or until a knife inserted into center comes out clean. Set cake aside and allow to cool.

6. While cake is baking, in a high-powered blender or coffee grinder, mix 2 cups coconut sugar and tapioca starch. Process until you have a fine powdery confectioners' sugar.

7. In a medium mixing bowl, combine coconut ghee and remaining ½ cup of cocoa powder, remaining vanilla, and confectioners' sugar; mix until well blended.

8. Add coconut cream; beat with a beater until fluffy. Icing should be smooth and not too thick, so that it can spread easily. If icing is too thick, add a little more coconut cream.

9. Remove cooled cake onto a plate; frost using a metal spatula. Slice, and serve.

PER SERVING Calories: 721 | Fat: 33g | Protein: 11g | Sodium: 345mg | Fiber: 8g | Carbohydrates: 105g

Chocolate Chip Coconut Cookies

Sometimes you just need a cookie! This low-carb recipe will give you a better-than-standard cookie-to-guilt ratio.

INGREDIENTS | MAKES 3 DOZEN

¼ cup coconut flour

3½ tablespoons tapioca starch

1 cup brown rice flour

½ teaspoon sea salt

1 teaspoon baking soda

1¼ cups unrefined coconut sugar

½ cup shredded coconut

1 cup coconut oil

2 eggs

2 tablespoons coconut milk

1½ teaspoons vanilla

1 (12-ounce) package semisweet chocolate chips

Coconut Sugar

Coconut sugar is made from the nectar of coconut flowers. Many people worry that because the flowers are being sacrificed to produce coconut sugar, using coconut sugar is damaging to the coconut tree. There is no reason to worry about this because coconut trees are in blossom regularly throughout the year, and are constantly producing new coconut fruit. Coconut sugar from properly harvested sap is a sustainable product. It is the producers who indiscriminately destroy all of the blossoms and fruit on the coconut tree to produce coconut sugar that is the problem.

1. Preheat the oven to 375°F.

2. In a mixing bowl, combine coconut flour, tapioca starch, rice flour, salt, and baking soda; mix well. Set aside.

3. With a hand mixer, cream together coconut sugar, shredded coconut, coconut oil, eggs, coconut milk, and vanilla. Beat until well mixed; add dry ingredients a little at a time until well combined.

4. Stir in chocolate chips; chill dough in the refrigerator for about 1 hour, or until firm.

5. Scoop dough onto well-greased baking sheet in 1" balls; bake for 8 minutes. Remove from the oven; allow cookies to cool on the cookie sheet for about 5 minutes before eating.

PER 1 COOKIE | Calories: 162 | Fat: 10g | Protein: 1g | Sodium: 74mg | Fiber: 1g | Carbohydrates: 18g

Strawberries with Coconut Shortcake

This is like classic strawberry shortcake—without as many carbs!

INGREDIENTS | SERVES 8

⅓ cup coconut oil, melted
6 eggs
¼ cup coconut sugar
½ teaspoon sea salt
½ teaspoon vanilla
½ cup coconut flour
½ teaspoon baking soda
2 pounds fresh strawberries
1 cup coconut cream, divided

1. Preheat the oven to 400°F. Grease a muffin pan; sprinkle with coconut flour, turning to coat evenly.

2. Mix coconut oil, eggs, sugar, salt, and vanilla.

3. Add coconut flour and baking soda to make a batter. Pour into muffin pan, filling each one about halfway.

4. Bake shortcakes for about 15 minutes, or until golden brown. Remove from oven; take shortcakes out of muffin pan with a fork. Allow to cool for 10–15 minutes before serving.

5. Wash, cap, and slice strawberries. Cut each shortcake in half; place ¼ cup of cut strawberries in the middle. Top with 2 tablespoons of coconut cream and a few more slices of strawberry. Serve.

PER SERVING Calories: 355 | Fat: 20g | Protein: 7g | Sodium: 289mg | Fiber: 5g | Carbohydrates: 40g

Coconut Cream Pie with Toasted Coconut Pecan Crust

This delicious coconut cream pie combines a traditional coconut milk pudding with a low-carb gluten-free pie crust.

INGREDIENTS | SERVES 6

1¼ cups plus 1 tablespoon shredded coconut, toasted

1 cup pecan pieces, chopped

½ cup coconut flour

¾ cup coconut sugar

2 teaspoons ground cinnamon plus 1 dash

⅓ cup coconut ghee

½ cup coconut sugar

¼ cup tapioca starch

2 cups unsweetened coconut milk

1 teaspoon vanilla

1 ripe mango, peeled, pitted, and diced

Coconut and IBS

Many people have experienced relief from their irritable bowel syndrome (IBS) after beginning to use coconut daily. What a tasty cure for a nasty problem! Although little research has been done, anecdotal evidence suggests that just two coconut macaroons can knock out a bout of IBS- or Crohn's-related diarrhea. This may have something to do with coconut's ability to absorb large amounts of liquid.

1. In a food processor, pulse 1 cup of shredded coconut with pecans, coconut flour, sugar, and 2 teaspoons cinnamon until it has the consistency of coarse sand.

2. Add ghee; pulse several more times, or until crumbly and mixture begins to fall away from the sides of the bowl.

3. Scoop crumbs out into a large pie pan; spread evenly over the bottom of the pan, using fingers to press crumbs across the bottom and up the sides.

4. Bake crust for 8 minutes at 375°F; remove from oven. Set aside to cool.

5. In a medium saucepan over medium heat, whisk together sugar, tapioca starch, and coconut milk. Bring to a boil, stirring constantly, and cook 1–2 minutes, or until thickened. Remove from heat and allow to cool about 3–5 minutes.

6. Stir in vanilla, a dash of cinnamon, and ¼ cup shredded coconut; stir well, and pour coconut filling into the crust. Top with diced mango and sprinkle with remaining tablespoon of toasted coconut; chill for 1 hour before serving.

PER SERVING Calories: 720 | Fat: 49g | Protein: 5g | Sodium: 61mg | Fiber: 8g | Carbohydrates: 73g

Coconut Whipped Cream Topping

This easy-to-make coconut cream topping is delicious with Strawberries with Coconut Shortcake (see recipe in this chapter).

INGREDIENTS | SERVES 6

1 cup coconut cream
⅓ cup coconut sugar
1 tablespoon vanilla
¼ cup coconut flour

Coconut and Candida

Because coconut is highly antifungal in nature, it is a great weapon against candida. Candida is a systemic yeast infection that can overrun every system in the body. Coconut's medium-chain fatty acids are easily absorbed into the cells of the body, where they can kill yeast overgrowth and boost your immune system. If you have candida, avoid sugars as much as possible and eat at least 2 tablespoons of coconut oil a day.

1. Chill coconut cream, covered, in a stainless steel mixing bowl overnight. Beat until thick and fluffy.

2. In a high-powered blender or a coffee grinder, process sugar until it reaches a fine powdery consistency.

3. To the beaten coconut cream, add vanilla; beat in powdered sugar and coconut flour a little at a time, until topping reaches the desired consistency.

PER SERVING Calories: 201 | Fat: 14g | Protein: 2g | Sodium: 2mg | Fiber: 3g | Carbohydrates: 17g

Key Lime Coconut Bars

Key Lime Coconut Bars are a great bake sale item.

INGREDIENTS | **MAKES 12**

½ cup shredded sweetened coconut

¾ cups coconut flour

¼ cup coconut sugar

5 tablespoons coconut ghee, chilled

3 large egg yolks

1 can coconut cream

2 tablespoons tapioca starch

4 teaspoons grated key lime zest, plus more for garnish

1 cup lime juice

1. Preheat the oven to 350°F.

2. Spread shredded coconut on a parchment-lined baking sheet; bake for about 5 minutes, stirring every 2 minutes, until golden brown. Remove from oven and cool; set aside.

3. In a mixing bowl, mix coconut flour, coconut sugar, and half of the toasted coconut. Using a pastry cutter, cut the ghee into the coconut flour mixture until it is crumbly. Pat into the bottom of a 9" × 13" baking pan; bake 20 minutes, or until golden brown. Cool slightly.

4. In a medium saucepan over medium heat, beat together egg yolks, coconut cream, tapioca starch, 4 teaspoons of lime zest, and lime juice. Bring to a boil; cook about 1 minute, until thickened. Remove from heat.

5. Pour filling into cooled crust; sprinkle with remaining toasted coconut. Bake another 10 minutes; remove from oven. Chill until ready to serve. Before serving, dust with powdered sugar and sprinkle with lime zest.

PER SERVING Calories: 253 | Fat: 14g | Protein: 2g | Sodium: 24mg | Fiber: 3g | Carbohydrates: 31g

Coconut Oatmeal Cookie Bars

These Coconut Oatmeal Cookie Bars really reduce the carbs as compared to the classic oatmeal cookie.

INGREDIENTS | MAKES 12

¼ cup coconut flour

¼ cup coconut sugar

¼ cup rolled oats

¼ cup shredded coconut

¼ cup coconut oil

1 egg

½ teaspoon baking soda

Young Versus Mature Coconuts

Young coconuts are softer and sweeter, and tend to be used for coconut water and meat. Mature coconuts are dry and hard, and are used to make coconut milk and coconut oil. A young coconut's flesh is tender enough to scoop out with a spoon, while a mature coconut's flesh is hard and can be broken up into chunks. Depending on where you live, you may need to seek out young coconuts in a specialty store.

1. Preheat the oven to 350°F.

2. In a mixing bowl, combine coconut flour, sugar, oats, and shredded coconut.

3. Melt coconut oil; add egg and baking soda. Mix well into dry ingredients.

4. Drop by spoonfuls onto a greased cookie sheet; bake for about 10–12 minutes, or until lightly browned at the edges. Remove from oven, and cool on a wire rack.

PER SERVING Calories: 126 | Fat: 5g | Protein: 1g | Sodium: 57mg | Fiber: 1g | Carbohydrates: 20g

Sweet Potato Pudding

This sweet potato pudding is a delicious way to get your beta-carotene!

INGREDIENTS | SERVES 6

1½ cups coconut milk

1 cup coconut sugar

¾ pounds sweet potatoes, peeled and finely grated

2 tablespoons golden raisins

1 tablespoon coconut oil

2 teaspoons vanilla

¼ teaspoon ground ginger

⅛ teaspoon ground cinnamon

1 dash salt

1. Preheat the oven to 350°F. Grease an 8" × 8" baking dish; set aside.

2. In a large mixing bowl, combine coconut milk and sugar; stir until dissolved.

3. Add sweet potatoes, raisins, coconut oil, vanilla, ginger, cinnamon, and salt; mix well. Pour into greased baking dish; bake for 1 hour.

4. Reduce heat to 250°F; bake 1 more hour, until a golden crust forms and a knife inserted in the center comes out mostly clean. Remove from oven; cover and refrigerate for 3 days before serving. Serve chilled.

PER SERVING Calories: 322 | Fat: 14g | Protein: 2g | Sodium: 55mg | Fiber: 2g | Carbohydrates: 49g

Coconut Crème Brûlée

Coconut Crème Brûlée is a beautiful dessert. Serve it at your next dinner party or holiday celebration.

INGREDIENTS | SERVES 6

½ cup plus 6 teaspoons coconut sugar
6 large egg yolks
1 large egg
2 cups heavy whipping cream
⅔ cup unsweetened coconut milk
⅔ cup shredded sweetened coconut
Water, as needed

1. Preheat the oven to 350°F. Place 6 ramekins in large roasting pan.

2. In a large bowl, beat ½ cup sugar, egg yolks, and whole egg.

3. In a medium saucepan over medium heat, add cream, coconut milk, and shredded coconut; bring to boil. Whisk in egg mixture. Pour custard into ramekins, dividing equally.

4. Pour enough hot water into roasting pan to come halfway up sides of cups, about 2". Bake 35–40 minutes, or until custards are just set in center. Remove from water; cool, and chill overnight.

5. Before serving, preheat broiler and arrange ramekins on a baking sheet. Sprinkle 1 teaspoon of sugar evenly over each custard. Broil until sugar browns, watching closely, for about 2 minutes; chill for at least 1 hour.

PER SERVING Calories: 518 | Fat: 44g | Protein: 6g | Sodium: 80mg | Fiber: 0g | Carbohydrates: 29g

Vegan

Tomato-Coconut Curry Soup

This spicy tomato soup is perfect for those cold winter days!

INGREDIENTS | SERVES 6

1 tablespoon coconut oil
1 small onion, minced
1 tablespoon vegan red curry paste
1 (28-ounce) can peeled whole Italian plum tomatoes
1 (14-ounce) can coconut milk
1 cup chopped portobello mushrooms
½ pound firm chickpea curd, drained and cubed
2 tablespoons raw coconut sugar
Juice of 1 lime
2 tablespoons fresh basil

1. In a medium saucepan, heat coconut oil over medium heat; add onion and red curry paste. Sauté 5 minutes, or until onion is translucent and curry is dissolved.

2. In a food processor, purée tomatoes and add to the saucepan with onions.

3. Add coconut milk and mushrooms; bring to a boil and reduce heat to medium-low. Simmer 5 minutes.

4. Add chickpea curd, sugar, lime juice, and basil; simmer another 5 minutes, or until heated through.

PER SERVING Calories: 219 | Fat: 17g | Protein: 6g | Sodium: 221mg | Fiber: 2g | Carbohydrates: 14g

Chickpea Curd

Even if you can find tofu made from non-gmo soy, soy should only be used in small amounts, if at all. Soy is one of the most common allergens, and many people have sensitivities to it and can suffer a variety of symptoms from hot flashes to gastrointestinal discomfort, even when eating only small amounts. Chickpea curd or Burmese tofu is a traditional food of Myanmar. It is high in protein, and can be used just like tofu in any recipes that call for it.

Coconut Mashed Sweet Potatoes

Mashed sweet potatoes with ginger and coconut milk taste delicious, and they're good for you!

INGREDIENTS | SERVES 6

3 pounds sweet potatoes
1 cup coconut milk
1 tablespoon fresh ginger, grated
½ teaspoon sea salt

Anti-Inflammatory Properties of Coconut

Coconut has anti-inflammatory properties that help reduce inflammation in conditions like inflammatory bowel diseases, such as Crohn's disease and arthritis.

1. Preheat the oven to 400°F.

2. Prick sweet potatoes with a fork several times; bake for 45 minutes to 1 hour, or until potatoes can be easily pierced with a fork.

3. Remove from oven; allow potatoes to cool enough to be handled. Peel and discard skin; transfer to a mixing bowl and mash with a potato masher.

4. Add coconut milk and ginger; stir well. Scoop into a casserole dish.

5. Reduce oven to 350°F; bake 10 minutes, or until heated through. Season with salt. Serve hot.

PER SERVING Calories: 247 | Fat: 8g | Protein: 4g | Sodium: 260mg | Fiber: 6g | Carbohydrates: 41g

Coconut Rice Pudding

Rice pudding is a classic comfort food. This makes a great dessert—try it after a dinner of Mixed Vegetable Coconut Stew (see recipe in this chapter).

INGREDIENTS | SERVES 8

2 cups uncooked rice

½ cup coconut yogurt

7 cups water

3 cups coconut milk

⅔ cup raw coconut sugar

2 tablespoons coconut oil

½ cup golden raisins, chopped

1 teaspoon real vanilla

1 teaspoon cinnamon, divided

1 cup coconut flakes

1. In a medium mixing bowl, combine rice, yogurt, and 3 cups water; allow to soak at room temperature overnight.

2. In a medium saucepan over medium-high heat, bring rice to a boil in remaining 4 cups water; cover and reduce heat to medium-low. Simmer for 15 minutes, or until rice can be fluffed with a fork.

3. Add coconut milk, sugar, coconut oil, raisins, and vanilla; simmer for another 20 minutes over medium-low heat, stirring occasionally. Add cinnamon; remove from heat.

4. In a dry medium skillet, toast coconut flakes until edges begin to turn golden brown. Remove from heat; place in a serving dish. Spoon rice pudding into bowls, and top with additional cinnamon and toasted coconut. Serve hot or chilled.

PER SERVING Calories: 524 | Fat: 25g | Protein: 6g | Sodium: 46mg | Fiber: 2g | Carbohydrates: 71g

Vegan Coconut Macaroons

Try this vegan version of coconut macaroons—these are one of those things that you just can't live without!

INGREDIENTS | MAKES 2 DOZEN

1 cup coconut sugar
½ cup coconut milk
2 tablespoons maple syrup
2 teaspoons vanilla extract
1 teaspoon sea salt
3 cups shredded coconut
½ cup coconut flour

1. Preheat the oven to 350°F. Line a baking sheet with parchment paper.

2. In a medium mixing bowl, combine coconut sugar, coconut milk, maple syrup, vanilla, and salt. Add shredded coconut and coconut flour; mix well.

3. Using a basting brush, lightly grease parchment-lined baking sheet with coconut oil.

4. Form the mixture into 1" balls; place on parchment-lined baking sheet about 1" apart. Bake for 10 minutes, or until edges are golden brown.

PER 1 COOKIE | Calories: 110 | Fat: 5g | Protein: 1g | Sodium: 128mg | Fiber: 2g | Carbohydrates: 17g

Coconut Cream Pie

This coconut cream pie is a delicious dessert for entertaining, or for just because!

INGREDIENTS | MAKES 1 8" PIE

1½ cups shredded coconut

1 cup pecans, roughly chopped

¼ cup coconut flour

¾ cup coconut sugar

2 teaspoons cinnamon plus additional for dusting

¼ cup coconut oil

1 tablespoon potato starch flour

¼ teaspoon sea salt

2 cups coconut milk

1 teaspoon vanilla

Coconut Flour

Coconut flour is the finely ground, dehydrated, mature coconut meat. Coconut flour does not contain gluten, and is very high in protein, so it is good for gluten-free foods and for people who are trying to cut carbohydrates to a minimum. Coconut flour absorbs a lot more liquid than other flours, which is why a recipe with coconut flour may only call for ¼ cup of flour and a larger number of eggs, which also work to hold the finished product together. Baked goods made with coconut flour are much more crumbly than those made with wheat flours.

1. Preheat the oven to 375°F.

2. In a food processor, pulse 1 cup coconut, pecans, coconut flour, ½ cup sugar, and 2 teaspoons cinnamon until mixture is finely chopped and well mixed.

3. Add coconut oil; pulse several more times until mixture is crumbly.

4. Press into the bottom of a 9" pie pan; bake crust for 8–10 minutes, or until golden brown.

5. In a medium saucepan, mix remaining sugar, potato starch flour, and salt. Turn burner on to medium heat; whisk in coconut milk. Stirring constantly, cook over medium heat until mixture thickens and comes to a boil, about 5 minutes.

6. Remove from heat; stir in vanilla. Pour into pie crust; dust with cinnamon and remaining ½ cup shredded coconut. Chill, and serve cold.

PER ⅛TH OF PIE | Calories: 447 | Fat: 35g | Protein: 3g | Sodium: 126mg | Fiber: 4g | Carbohydrates: 35g

Thai Curried Chickpeas with Rice

These curried chickpeas with coconut go great with flatbread.

INGREDIENTS | SERVES 6

1 cup dried chickpeas
7½ cups water
2 tablespoons coconut oil
1½ cups uncooked rice
1¾ cups coconut milk
Sea salt, to taste
1 tablespoon onion, chopped
4 cloves garlic, pressed
2 tablespoons red curry paste
2 teaspoons coconut aminos
1 medium tomato, diced
Juice of 1 lime
1 tablespoon fresh basil leaves, chopped

Coconut Aminos

Coconut aminos is a sauce made from fermented coconut, in much the same process that soy sauce is made. Coconut aminos are a much healthier alternative to soy sauce, since most soy sauce is made with genetically modified soybeans, and soy is one of the most common allergens.

1. In a bowl, add chickpeas and 3 cups water. Soak dried chickpeas overnight. The next day, drain and rinse chickpeas and add to a medium pot with another 3 cups of water. Bring to a boil, then reduce heat to medium. Simmer for 15 minutes, or until beans are soft; set aside.

2. In a large saucepan over medium, heat 1 tablespoon oil. Add rice; cook 2 minutes.

3. Add 1½ cups coconut milk and 1½ cups water. Bring to a boil and reduce heat to medium-low; cover and simmer for 15 minutes. Remove from heat; add salt to taste, and set aside.

4. In a medium skillet, heat 1 tablespoon coconut oil; add onions and garlic. Sauté 5 minutes, or until onion is translucent.

5. Add curry paste; mix until curry is dissolved in oil.

6. Add chickpeas, coconut aminos, tomato, and lime juice; bring to a boil, then reduce heat to low. Simmer for 5 minutes.

7. Add remaining coconut milk; cook another 2 minutes, or until warmed through. Stir in basil; remove from heat. Serve with rice.

PER SERVING Calories: 475 | Fat: 21g | Protein: 12g | Sodium: 60mg | Fiber: 7g | Carbohydrates: 62g

Mixed Vegetable Coconut Stew

This savory vegetable stew has a wide variety of vegetables for a power-packed meal!

1. In a large soup pot, heat coconut oil; add onion and sauté for 5 minutes, or until translucent.

2. Add turnips, sweet potato, and pumpkin; cover and cook over medium heat for 5 more minutes.

3. Add marjoram, ginger, cinnamon, salt, and pepper; simmer, stirring occasionally, for another 10 minutes.

4. Add vegetable stock, almonds, jalapeño, and sugar; simmer another 10–15 minutes, or until vegetables are tender. Remove from heat; stir in creamed coconut. Serve hot.

PER SERVING Calories: 184 | Fat: 13g | Protein: 3g | Sodium: 669mg | Fiber: 3g | Carbohydrates: 18g

Infection-Fighting Powers of Coconut

Coconut has amazing antimicrobial properties! The medium-chain fatty acids and high lauric acid content of coconut oil can deactivate microbes by changing their lipid structure, thereby rendering them powerless to attack your body.

Carrot Coconut Bisque

This Carrot Coconut Bisque can be served hot or cold.

INGREDIENTS | SERVES 6

10 medium carrots, sliced
1 tablespoon coconut oil
½ cup shallots, minced
½ teaspoon white pepper
1 teaspoon sea salt
1 teaspoon potato starch flour
1 cup vegetable stock
2 cups coconut milk
½ cup fresh basil, finely chopped
½ teaspoon ground nutmeg

1. In a steamer over medium heat, cook carrots until soft, about 10 minutes.

2. In a large soup pot, heat coconut oil; add shallots, pepper, and salt. Sauté for 5 minutes, or until shallots are tender. Sprinkle in potato starch flour and whisk in stock; stir constantly until mixture thickens and comes to a boil, about 3 minutes.

3. In a food processor, add stock mixture and steamed carrots; purée until smooth.

4. Add coconut milk; process until well mixed, and return to pot.

5. Stir in basil and nutmeg; heat on low, stirring occasionally for 1 minute, or until heated through. Serve hot, or chill and serve cold.

PER SERVING Calories: 225 | Fat: 19g | Protein: 3g | Sodium: 626mg | Fiber: 3g | Carbohydrates: 15g

Potato Leek Soup with Coconut Milk

Potato soup with leeks is a classic comfort food. Curl up in front of the fire with this and a piece of crusty bread, and you will think you died and went to heaven!

INGREDIENTS | SERVES 6

1 tablespoon coconut oil

2 cloves garlic, pressed

2 medium leeks, white parts only, sliced

5 medium Yukon Gold potatoes, peeled and cubed

4 cups vegetable stock

1 teaspoon dried oregano

½ teaspoon black pepper

½ teaspoon sea salt

1 dash cayenne

1 (14-ounce) can coconut milk

1. In a large soup pot over medium, heat oil. Add garlic and leeks; sauté about 5 minutes, or until leeks are soft.

2. Add the potatoes, vegetable stock, oregano, pepper, salt, and cayenne. Bring to a boil; reduce heat to medium-low and simmer for 10–15 minutes, or until potatoes are soft.

3. Add coconut milk. Carefully pour soup into a food processor; pulse several times, until soup is puréed.

4. Pour back into soup pot; simmer another 5 minutes. Remove from heat, and serve hot.

PER SERVING Calories: 300 | Fat: 16g | Protein: 5g | Sodium: 652mg | Fiber: 5g | Carbohydrates: 39g

Going Raw

Coconut Butter

This raw coconut butter makes a delicious spread.

INGREDIENTS | MAKES 2 CUPS

2 cups unsweetened shredded coconut

How to Shred Coconut

To make freshly shredded coconut, open, drain, and crack a mature coconut, separating the shell from the chunks of coconut meat. Use a box grater to shred the coconut meat; it is not necessary to have a special coconut grater. Whether you use the coarse or fine side of the grater is a matter of personal preference, depending on the recipe or what you are using the coconut for.

In a food processor, purée coconut for 10–20 minutes. Use a spatula to scrape coconut butter into a glass jar. Store in the refrigerator.

PER 1 TABLESPOON Calories: 6 | Fat: 1g | Protein: 0g | Sodium: 1mg | Fiber: 0g | Carbohydrates: 1g

Raw Chocolate Coconut Truffles

These raw chocolate truffles are a great way to satisfy your sweet tooth and get the great benefits of raw coconut oil at the same time.

INGREDIENTS | MAKES 12

4 large dates
3 tablespoons water
½ cup raw cacao powder
1 cup raw shredded coconut plus ¼ cup
2 tablespoons raw coconut oil
½ teaspoon cinnamon
½ teaspoon vanilla
1 dash sea salt

Eating Raw

Many people have experienced great healing by switching to a raw food diet. A raw food diet has been credited for weight loss, preventing gray hair and wrinkles, staving off osteoporosis, reducing cravings, and promoting a healthy glow to the skin. On the other hand, there are many foods that benefit from cooking. Spinach and kale, and cruciferous vegetables like cabbage and broccoli, benefit from light steaming because they contain goitrogens that when eaten raw can put a lot of stress on the thyroid. If you have a weak thyroid and want to stay 100 percent raw, you may want to replace these with other types of leafy greens like dulse, romaine lettuce, chard, and red or green leaf lettuce.

1. Remove pits from dates; in a food processor, process dates and water to form a paste. Using a spatula, scrape mixture out into a large bowl. Stir in cacao powder.

2. In the food processor, mix 1 cup shredded coconut and coconut oil; process until a thick paste forms.

3. Add date paste; purée until smooth, then add cinnamon, vanilla, and sea salt. Mix well.

4. Form mixture into 1" balls; roll in remaining grated coconut. Place on a parchment-paper-lined baking sheet; refrigerate for 30 minutes before serving.

PER 1 TRUFFLE | Calories: 120 | Fat: 9g | Protein: 2g | Sodium: 12mg | Fiber: 4g | Carbohydrates: 11g

Raw Coconut Ice Cream

Raw coconut ice cream is delicious, and good for you!

INGREDIENTS | SERVES 6

2 cups raw cashews

3½ cups filtered water plus additional as needed

2 cups young coconut meat

1 cup raw honey

¼ cup Coconut Butter (see recipe in this chapter)

2 tablespoons vanilla extract

½ vanilla bean

½ teaspoon sea salt

1. In a medium mixing bowl, add cashews and 3 cups water. Soak overnight; drain and set aside.

2. In a food processor, purée ½ cup water, coconut meat, honey, Coconut Butter, vanilla extract, vanilla bean seeds, and salt until smooth.

3. Add cashews and additional water, as needed; process until smooth. Freeze in an ice cream maker according to the manufacturer's directions.

PER SERVING Calories: 528 | Fat: 27g | Protein: 9g | Sodium: 205mg | Fiber: 4g | Carbohydrates: 70g

Coconut Milk and Cream

Making your own raw coconut milk and cream ensures quality and saves money.

INGREDIENTS | **MAKES 2½ CUPS COCONUT MILK AND ½ CUP COCONUT CREAM**

1 mature coconut (about 1 cup coconut meat and 1 cup coconut water)
2 cups warm water

1. Using a hammer and awl, puncture 2 of the eyes in the top of the coconut; pour out coconut water.

2. Wrap the coconut in a hand towel; use a hammer to break the coconut into pieces. Place coconut pieces into a bowl; sort out the brown pieces of shell and discard.

3. In a food processor, process coconut meat with coconut water and ½ cup water. Pour off coconut milk; add remaining 1½ cups of warm water, and again, pour off coconut milk.

4. Strain milk using a fine sieve. Allow milk to sit overnight in the refrigerator and the cream will rise to the top, where you can skim it off for later use if desired.

PER 1 CUP COCONUT MILK (coconut cream separated)
Calories: 90 | Fat: 5g | Protein: 1g | Sodium: 30mg | Fiber: 0g | Carbohydrates: 10g

PER 1 TABLESPOON COCONUT CREAM Calories: 49 | Fat: 5g | Protein: 1g | Sodium: 1mg | Fiber: 0g | Carbohydrates: 1g

Orange Roughy with Fruit and Coconut Cream

This recipe is a beautiful and delicious way to entertain guests!

INGREDIENTS | SERVES 6

6 orange roughy fillets

Juice of 6 limes, divided

1 large onion, finely chopped

2 mangoes, peeled and pitted, cut into bite-sized pieces

½ pound strawberries, cut into bite-sized pieces

2 cups melon of your choice, cubed

1 batch Coconut Cream Mayonnaise (see Chapter 20)

1. Cut fillets into ½" strips.

2. Set aside 1 tablespoon of lime juice; mix remaining juice and chopped onion. Add fish strips, stirring lightly to coat. Cover; marinate in the refrigerator overnight.

3. Remove marinated fish from the refrigerator; drain. Serve with fruit and Coconut Cream Mayonnaise (see Chapter 20).

PER SERVING Calories: 620 | Fat: 52g | Protein: 18g | Sodium: 88mg | Fiber: 4g | Carbohydrates: 28g

Raw Fermented Fish

Many cultures have traditionally prepared raw fermented fish. Historically, sushi was made from fermented raw fish. In the Inuit culture, fish was fermented by digging a hole in the ground, placing freshly caught fish inside the hole, and then covering it with earth. It fermented for 2–3 weeks or longer, depending on preference. The fish was then unearthed, and eaten frozen. Some other traditional fermented raw-fish dishes are Norwegian rakfisk, Swedish surströmming, and Egyptian fesikh.

Coconut, Carrot, and Ginger Soup

This raw coconut soup with carrots and ginger is packed with vitamins!

INGREDIENTS | SERVES 6

¼" piece gingerroot

1 orange bell pepper

4 carrots

2 tablespoons lime juice

¼ cup raw cashews

1 mango, peeled, pitted, and cubed

1 cup water

1 teaspoon raw honey

2 tablespoons coconut oil

Sea salt, to taste

Shredded coconut, for garnish

1. In a food processor, process all ingredients except shredded coconut until smooth.

2. Pour into a covered container; chill overnight. Pour into bowls; sprinkle with coconut. Serve cold.

PER SERVING Calories: 118 | Fat: 7g | Protein: 2g | Sodium: 30mg | Fiber: 2g | Carbohydrates: 14g

Does Coconut Need to be Soaked?

Coconut is much lower in phytic acid than tree nuts and other seeds. Soaking will certainly not hurt, and if you are extremely sensitive to the effects of phytic acid, it certainly won't hurt to err on the safe side by soaking your coconut. Otherwise, it is a matter of personal preference.

Raw Nut Butter with Coconut Oil

Raw nut butters are nutrient-dense and delicious.

INGREDIENTS | **MAKES 1 CUP**

1 cup raw nuts or seeds of your choice
1 tablespoon coconut oil

Coconut Oil as Sunscreen?

Did you know that coconut oil can protect you from harmful effects of the sun? Applying coconut oil to your skin regularly not only acts as a wonderful skin conditioner, it also helps protect your skin from sunburn and harmful UV radiation.

1. In a food processor, chop nuts or seeds to a fine powder.

2. Add coconut oil, a little at a time, until nut butter reaches the desired consistency. Store in the refrigerator.

PER 1 TABLESPOON | Calories: 59 | Fat: 5g | Protein: 2g | Sodium: 0mg | Fiber: 1g | Carbohydrates: 2g

Lacto-Fermented Coconut

Lacto-fermented coconut is a tasty way to get probiotics into your diet, and is a great snack!

INGREDIENTS | SERVES 6

1 medium-sized raw coconut, cut into small pieces

4–5 green chilies

1 teaspoon cumin seeds

1 teaspoon mustard seeds

2 tablespoons coriander seeds

1½ teaspoons sea salt

2 sprigs curry leaves

¼ teaspoon turmeric powder

2–3 garlic cloves

2 cups coconut water

2–3 tablespoons coconut kefir

1. Pack coconut pieces, chilies, spices, and garlic into a glass jar.

2. Mix coconut water and kefir. Pour into glass jar, leaving ½" headspace. Cover and allow to ferment at room temperature for 24–48 hours. Cover and store in the refrigerator.

PER SERVING Calories: 323 | Fat: 30g | Protein: 4g | Sodium: 600mg | Fiber: 8g | Carbohydrates: 16g

Is Coconut a Nut?

Many people with tree nut allergies want to know if coconut is a tree nut and therefore dangerous to eat. Coconuts are not actually nuts, and though there are allergies to coconut, they are much less common than tree nut allergies. Coconuts are a type of fruit known as a drupe and are not closely related to other types of tree nuts.

CHAPTER 20

Dressings, Salsas, Sauces, and Beverages

Coconut Sour Cream

This thicker version of cultured coconut milk can be used as sour cream. This tangy treat is much better for you than the dairy version!

INGREDIENTS | YIELDS 1 CUP

1½ cups cultured coconut milk

1. Fold a piece of cheesecloth so it is 4 layers thick. Place over a small bowl, and add cultured coconut milk on top.

2. Stir every hour, until ½ cup of the "whey" has been strained out. Serve with recipes that call for sour cream, or store in the refrigerator.

PER 1 TABLESPOON Calories: 16 | Fat: 1g | Protein: 0g | Sodium: 1mg | Fiber: 0g | Carbohydrates: 2g

Coconut Cream Mayonnaise

This probiotic coconut mayonnaise is a condiment that not only gives you healthy fats you can feel good about eating, it is delicious and helps you digest your food— the way old-fashioned condiments were meant to!

INGREDIENTS | **MAKES 2 CUPS**

1 egg
1 tablespoon fresh whey
1 teaspoon mustard powder
1 tablespoon lime juice
Sea salt and black pepper, to taste
¾ cup coconut oil
¼ cup sunflower seed oil
1 cup coconut cream

1. In a blender, mix egg, whey, mustard powder, lime juice, and a dash of salt and pepper. Allow to sit until ingredients are at room temperature.

2. Warm the coconut oil to melt; add sunflower seed oil and mix well. With the blender on high speed, add oil to the blender in a slow, steady stream until the mayonnaise is thickened and smooth.

3. Add coconut cream; blend until well mixed. Let mayonnaise sit at room temperature for 15 minutes to allow the active cultures in the whey to multiply, adding probiotic properties to your fresh mayonnaise. Place Coconut Cream Mayonnaise in the refrigerator, and chill for at least 1 hour before using.

PER 1 TABLESPOON | Calories: 86 | Fat: 10g | Protein: 0g | Sodium: 3mg | Fiber: 0g | Carbohydrates: 1g

Honey Coconut Mustard

One of the most satisfying things to make from scratch are condiments that you can have on hand that have been made by yourself from real, wholesome ingredients.

INGREDIENTS | MAKES 1 CUP

2 tablespoons fresh whey

½ cup pure water

¼ cup whole mustard seed

1 small turmeric root

½ teaspoon sea salt

¾ cup coconut water vinegar

1 tablespoon honey

Whey

Adding fresh whey to your condiments changes them from just seasonings to powerful probiotic digestive aids. To get liquid whey, simply pour out the liquid that separates from plain yogurt or kefir, or make your own by mixing a 1 tablespoon of plain yogurt with active cultures into 2 cups of fresh unpasteurized milk and letting it sit at room temperature overnight, or until it begins to separate. The clear liquid is the whey.

1. In a small mixing bowl, mix 1 tablespoon whey, water, and mustard seed. Cover, and allow to stand overnight on your countertop.

2. In the morning, strain mustard seed through a fine sieve; rinse.

3. Wearing rubber gloves, peel turmeric root; slice.

4. Add mustard seed, turmeric root, and salt to your food processor with the vinegar. Process until smooth, adding additional water, if needed, until it has a mustard consistency.

5. Remove mustard mixture from the processor into a small saucepan. Bring mixture to a boil; remove from heat and cool.

6. Add remaining whey and 1 tablespoon of honey, or to taste; mix well. Allow mustard to sit at room temperature for at least 15 minutes before moving to your refrigerator.

PER 1 TABLESPOON | Calories: 21 | Fat: 1g | Protein: 1g | Sodium: 75mg | Fiber: 0g | Carbohydrates: 3g

Thai Peanut and Coconut Dipping Sauce

This classic Thai dipping sauce is a great way to add antioxidants to your meal.

INGREDIENTS | MAKES 2 CUPS

½ cup coconut cream

⅓ cup hot water

½ cup peanuts, roughly chopped

1 teaspoon fish sauce

1 small bird's eye chili, chopped

½ teaspoon curry powder

Juice of 1 lime

1 tablespoon chopped cilantro

1. Mix coconut cream and hot water; pour into food processor.

2. Add peanuts, fish sauce, chili, curry powder, and lime juice; process until smooth.

3. Stir in cilantro. Serve with shrimp or raw vegetables.

PER SERVING Calories: 26 | Fat: 2g | Protein: 1g | Sodium: 15mg | Fiber: 0g | Carbohydrates: 1g

Coconut and Cancer

Medical research has shown coconut oil to be protective against cancer! Coconut has unique antioxidant properties. It has also been shown to prevent the spreading of cancer, and boosts the immune system.

Mango Coconut Salsa

Mango Coconut Salsa is yummy with chicken quesadillas.

INGREDIENTS | **MAKES 2½ CUPS**

¼ cup green onions, thinly sliced

¼ cup fresh cilantro, chopped

1 teaspoon jalapeño, minced

1 large mango, peeled, pitted, and diced

¼ cup red bell pepper, finely diced

1 tablespoon lime juice

¼ cup shredded coconut

Sea salt, to taste

In a food processor, pulse all ingredients together until coarsely chopped and well mixed. Pour into a glass jar and cover. Refrigerate overnight before serving with chicken or fish.

PER ¼ CUP SERVING | Calories: 24 | Fat: 1g | Protein: 0g | Sodium: 2mg | Fiber: 1g | Carbohydrates: 5g

Storing Coconut Oil

Coconut oil does not have to be refrigerated. Because of its structure, it is a very stable oil and can be stored at room temperature for up to five years if it is kept out of direct sunlight or heat. This long shelf life of coconut oil is one of the things that makes it so much more healthier than other vegetable oils. Most vegetable oils are very unstable and become rancid when they are exposed to heat, which is why you should not cook with them. Olive oil is the only other exception to this, and it still cannot withstand as much heat as coconut oil can for cooking.

Roasted Poblano and Coconut Salsa

Try this Roasted Poblano Salsa with coconut for a nice sweet and spicy combination!

INGREDIENTS | **MAKES 2½ CUPS**

3 poblano peppers
1 small red onion, sliced
4 Roma tomatoes, halved
¼ cup grated coconut
2 tablespoons fresh orange juice
¼ cup coconut oil
2 tablespoons cilantro, chopped
Sea salt and freshly ground black pepper, to taste

1. Roast poblano peppers on a hot grill; about 1 minute on each side. Remove skin and seeds, and dice.

2. In a food processor, combine the poblanos, onion, and tomatoes; pulse 2 or 3 times, until all ingredients are coarsely chopped and well mixed.

3. Add grated coconut, orange juice, coconut oil, cilantro, and salt and pepper, to taste; pour into a glass jar. Cover and refrigerate overnight.

4. Remove from refrigerator; bring to room temperature. Shake well before using.

PER ¼ CUP SERVING | Calories: 70 | Fat: 6g | Protein: 1g | Sodium: 3mg | Fiber: 1g | Carbohydrates: 4g

Lime and Coconut Dressing

Coconut and lime make a delicious, creamy dressing.

INGREDIENTS | **MAKES 2 CUPS**

1 cup fresh cilantro leaves, rinsed

Juice and zest of 1 lime

1 tablespoon coconut vinegar

1 cup coconut milk

1 tablespoon coconut sugar

2 tablespoons coconut oil

Sea salt, to taste

¼ teaspoon chili pepper flakes

1. In a food processor, mix all ingredients; process until smooth. Pour into a glass jar, and refrigerate overnight.

2. Remove from refrigerator; bring to room temperature. Shake well before using.

PER 1 TABLESPOON SERVING | Calories: 23 | Fat: 2g | Protein: 0g | Sodium: 1mg | Fiber: 0g | Carbohydrates: 1g

Are All Coconut Oils Equal?

Not all coconut oil is the same. You should look for extra-virgin coconut oil that has been processed as little as possible. Coconut products that have been made from dried coconut can have mold contamination, and coconut oils that are hydrogenated or partially hydrogenated have lost their healthy properties, so look into your source very carefully and read all of the labels before buying.

Fresh Mint Coconut Salad Dressing

Mint coconut dressing is tasty with a classic green side salad.

INGREDIENTS | SERVES 6

½ cup fresh mint leaves

Juice of 1 lime

3 tablespoons coconut oil, melted

½ cup coconut milk

¼ teaspoon sea salt

½ teaspoon freshly ground black pepper

½ ripe avocado

Coconut Vinegar

Coconut vinegar can be made from the sap of the coconut flower or by fermenting coconut water. It is very similar to balsamic vinegar or apple cider vinegar, and has the same alkalizing effect in the body. The best quality vinegars are raw, and contain the live vinegar "mother" cultures.

1. In a food processor, mix mint leaves, lime juice, coconut oil, coconut milk, salt, and pepper; process until smooth.

2. Add avocado; process 1 more minute. Pour dressing into a glass jar, and store in the refrigerator.

3. Remove from refrigerator; bring to room temperature. Shake well before using.

PER SERVING Calories: 128 | Fat: 13g | Protein: 1g | Sodium: 103mg | Fiber: 2g | Carbohydrates: 3g

Coconut Water Kefir

Coconut Water Kefir is a great way to get your probiotics in a nice refreshing drink.

INGREDIENTS | **MAKES 2 QUARTS**

½ gallon coconut water from young coconuts

½ cup water kefir grains

Coconut Water

Not all coconut water is sweet. Depending on the variety of coconut and the age of those coconuts, coconut water can be very plain tasting. If you want sweet coconut water or juice, you need to get it from young coconuts, where the coconut meat is tender enough to scoop out of the shell. The varieties of coconut best known for sweet coconut water are golden to orange in color when young.

1. Add all ingredients to a large half-gallon glass jar; allow to sit on the counter at room temperature for 24–48 hours.

2. Strain out kefir grains; set aside for the next batch. Serve cold.

PER 8 OUNCE SERVING | Calories: 44 | Fat: 0 | Protein: 0 | Sodium: 50mg | Fiber: 0 | Carbohydrates: 8

Coconut Milk Kefir

Enjoy coconut milk in a whole new way with this rich, creamy yogurt-like drink.

INGREDIENTS | MAKES 2 QUARTS

½ gallon coconut milk
½ cup milk kefir grains

Kefir Grains

Milk kefir grains are a symbiotic colony of bacteria and yeast resembling a cauliflower floret that originated in Eurasia. The history and origin of kefir grains is vague and has a rich tradition in Russian folklore, with many variations of how kefir came into being. Whatever way you spin it, the benefits of kefir are undisputable, ranging from slowing the growth of cancerous tumors to rebuilding the flora in your digestive tract.

1. Add all ingredients to a large half-gallon glass jar; mix well.

2. Allow to sit on the counter at room temperature for 24–48 hours. Strain out kefir grains; set aside for the next batch. Serve cold.

PER 8 OUNCE SERVING | Calories: 70 | Fat: 6g | Protein: 1g | Sodium: 5mg | Fiber: 3g | Carbohydrates: 6g

Coconut Banana Smoothie

This yummy coconut banana smoothie makes a good breakfast!

INGREDIENTS | SERVES 6

Juice from 12 oranges
2 cups coconut milk
2 cups coconut cream
2 ripe bananas
2 cups crushed ice

In a blender, mix all ingredients; blend until smooth. Serve cold.

PER SERVING Calories: 525 | Fat: 44g | Protein: 6g | Sodium: 15mg | Fiber: 3g | Carbohydrates: 34g

Coconut Milk Cocoa

This delicious coconut milk hot cocoa is the perfect way to celebrate the end of a cold winter day!

INGREDIENTS | SERVES 6

2 cups coconut milk

4 cups boiling water

¾ cup coconut sugar

6 tablespoons cocoa powder

1 teaspoon ground cinnamon

3 teaspoons vanilla

Health Benefits of Coconut

Coconut has a rich tradition in folk medicine. Coconut has been used to treat asthma, bronchitis, bruises, colds, flu, and gingivitis. Coconut also has antifungal properties, and can help get rid of athletes foot. Modern medicine has also begun to take notice of coconut's healing properties. Research studies published in medical journals have documented a wide range of health benefits. Coconut has been shown to kill viruses and harmful bacteria, feed the brain, boost energy and endurance, and stabilize blood sugar levels with no side effects.

In a heavy-bottomed medium-sized saucepan over medium heat, mix coconut milk, water, sugar, cocoa powder, and cinnamon. Stir until all ingredients are dissolved and well mixed. Remove from heat, and add vanilla. Serve hot.

PER SERVING Calories: 264 | Fat: 17g | Protein: 3g | Sodium: 11mg | Fiber: 2g | Carbohydrates: 31g

Coconut Water

Coconut water is a refreshing sports drink with natural electrolytes that rehydrate and nourish the body!

INGREDIENTS | SERVES 6

4 young coconuts

Amazing Coconut Water

Coconut water is one of the purest liquids on the face of the earth. It is refreshing, and also has some amazing properties—it can help break up kidney stones and kill parasites, but it can also substitute for blood plasma! Because coconut water has very similar properties to blood plasma, it mixes very easily with blood, and in an extreme emergency, can be used for a blood transfusion. There are recorded incidents of soldiers during World War II receiving coconut water "blood" transfusions and living to tell about it later.

Open coconuts and pour out water; chill. Serve cold.

PER 8 OUNCE SERVING | Calories: 46 | Fat: 0g | Protein: 2g | Sodium: 252mg | Fiber: 3g | Carbohydrates: 9g

Coconut Milk

Coconut milk is easy to make—just blend and strain.

INGREDIENTS | MAKES 6 CUPS

3 mature coconuts

3 cups coconut water

1. Open coconuts; drain water. Cut meat into 1" chunks.

2. In a heavy-duty blender, combine coconut water and coconut meat. Blend on high speed until meat is puréed, adding additional water if needed.

3. Strain mixture through linen or a fine sieve. Chill, and serve or use in recipes that call for coconut milk.

PER 1 CUP SERVING | Calories: 445 | Fat: 48g | Protein: 5g | Sodium: 29mg | Fiber: 0g | Carbohydrates: 6g

Sample Weekly Menu Plans

The following weekly menus are guides to help you design and plan meals. Feel free to make substitutions or additions according to your health condition or what you have in your pantry. Leftover meals are also great to use later in the week. Dessert for late afternoon snack or after dinner is optional.

▼ SAMPLE FAMILY MENU PLAN

Weekday	Breakfast	Lunch	Snack	Dinner
Sunday	Fluffy Coconut Pancakes; Coconut Pancake Syrup; cut fruit; Coconut Scramble	Carrot Ginger Coconut Soup; green salad; Lime and Coconut Dressing	Coconut Spinach-Artichoke Dip and Pita Chips	Baking Powder Biscuits; Coconut Chicken Alfredo; Vegetable Medley with Coconut-Vinegar Butter Sauce
Monday	Hawaiian Sunrise Green Smoothie; Fishing Boat Breakfast	Sweet Potato Coconut Salad; Jamaican Coconut Corn Bread; Pea Tendrils with Coconut	Garlic Herb Coconut Crackers; Coconut-Cashew Shrimp Balls	Coconut Rice; Coconut Beef Stir-Fry; steamed vegetables
Tuesday	Fruit and Coconut Parfait; cheese omelet; Crispy Coconut Hash Brown Potatoes	Fish Roe with Coconut; Fruit Salad with Coconut Dressing	Three-Layer Coconut-Shrimp-Cheese Spread	Pani PoPo (Samoan Coconut Rolls); Coconut-Lime Hawaiian Pulled Pork; Stir-Fried Coconut Green Beans
Wednesday	Coconut Fruit and Nut Oatmeal; ham; fried eggs	Coconut Curry Corn Soup	Coconut-Tuna Lettuce Cups	Brown rice; Roasted Coconut Chicken; Roasted-Coconut Lemon-Garlic-Ginger Carrots
Thursday	Honey Coconut Quinoa; fried eggs; banana	Seared Tuna Salad with Coconut Lime Dressing; Baking Powder Biscuits; green salad; Fresh Mint Coconut Salad Dressing	Coconut Banana Smoothie	Kalio Hati; Plantains in Coconut Milk; Pea Tendrils with Coconut
Friday	Country Fried Steak Strips; Coconut Pan-Fried Potatoes	Baked Salmon with Coconut Crust; Toasted Coconut Green Salad	Coconut Shrimp with Pineapple-Cilantro Dip	Coconut Rice; Indian Coconut Lamb Curry; Cabbage with Coconut Vinegar
Saturday	Breakfast Casserole; Banana and Coconut Breakfast Muffins	Spicy Sweet Potato and Coconut Soup; Coconut Teff Pita Bread	Caribbean Crab Dip; plantain chips	Spare Ribs with Honey Coconut Glaze; Coconut Garlic Roasted Cowboy Fries; Roasted Balsamic Brussels Sprouts

▼ SAMPLE VEGAN MENU PLAN

Weekday	Breakfast	Lunch	Snack	Dinner
Sunday	Cream of Buckwheat Cereal; vegan toast with Coconut Butter; fresh fruit	Mango Coconut Salad; steamed vegetables	Coconut Fruit Kebabs with Coconut Cream	Coconut Rice; Coconut Black Beans; Pea Tendrils with Coconut; Coconut Milk
Monday	Fluffy Coconut Waffles; Coconut Pancake Syrup; chickpea sausage; berries	Sweet Potato Fries; green salad; Fresh Mint Coconut Salad Dressing	Garlic Herb Coconut Crackers; Spicy Coconut Dipping Sauce	Baking Powder Biscuits; Tomato-Coconut Curry Soup; Asparagus in Coconut Milk
Tuesday	Nuts; Coconut Banana Smoothie; Crispy Coconut Hash Brown Potatoes	Coconut Ginger Salad; steamed greens; mixed fruit	Coconut Rice Pudding	Coconut Beef Stir-Fry; Stir-Fried Coconut Green Beans; Coconut Water Kefir; Coconut Cream Pie
Wednesday	Hawaiian Sunrise Green Smoothie; Coconut Milk Kefir	Carrot Coconut Bisque; fermented sauerkraut	Vegan Coconut Macaroons	Baking Powder Biscuits; Thai Curried Chickpeas with Rice; green salad; Lime and Coconut Dressing
Thursday	Coconut milk yogurt; granola; Coconut Milk Cocoa	Carrot Coconut Salad; Coconut Curry Corn Soup	Coconut milk yogurt; mixed berries	Coconut Black Beans; Coconut Mashed Sweet Potatoes; steamed vegetables
Friday	Fruit smoothie; quinoa with coconut milk	Mixed Vegetable Coconut Stew; green salad with berries and shredded coconut meat; Lime and Coconut Dressing	Raw Coconut Ice Cream	Carrot Coconut Bisque; Coconut Milk Kefir; Vegan Coconut Macaroons
Saturday	Cream of Buckwheat Cereal; diced banana; Coconut Milk	Potato Leek Soup with Coconut Milk; green salad	Granola; cut fruit	Roasted Balsamic Brussels Sprouts; Coconut Curry Corn Soup; Coconut Rice Pudding

▼ SAMPLE WEIGHT-LOSS MENU PLAN

Weekday	Breakfast	Lunch	Snack	Dinner
Sunday	Fish Roe with Coconut; Hawaiian Green Smoothie; fruit	Lacto-fermented vegetables, Coconut Herrings	Caribbean Crab Dip; pita chips; cut fruit	Roasted Coconut Chicken; brown rice, steamed vegetables
Monday	Cream of Buckwheat Cereal; sliced fruit and berries	Coconut-Tuna Lettuce Cups; fruit	Carrot Ginger Coconut Soup	Chicken Vindaloo; Coconut Rice; Asparagus in Coconut Milk
Tuesday	Fruit and Coconut Parfait; Coconut Scramble	Turkey wrap; green salad; Lime and Coconut Dressing	Coconut Spinach-Artichoke Dip and Pita Chips	Coconut-Lime Hawaiian Pulled Pork; Coconut Black Beans; green salad
Wednesday	Coconut Banana Smoothie with coconut oil; whole-grain toast	Orange Roughy with Fruit and Coconut Cream	Lacto-Fermented Coconut; fruit	Coconut Braised Beef; Coconut Garlic Mashed Potatoes, Stir-Fried Coconut Green Beans
Thursday	Blueberries; soaked raw nuts; eggs fried in coconut oil; Crispy Coconut Hash Brown Potatoes	Coconut Butternut Squash Chowder	Raw Coconut Ice Cream; strawberries	Indian Coconut Lamb Curry; Pea Tendrils with Coconut
Friday	Coconut Fruit and Nut Oatmeal; berries; Breakfast Casserole	Turkey avocado wraps	Coconut Banana Smoothie	Chicken Satay with Peanut Coconut Sauce; Roasted Balsamic Brussels Sprouts
Saturday	Coconut Milk Kefir; Coconut Rice with Mangoes	Thai Fish in Banana Leaf	Soaked nuts; apple slices with Coconut Butter	Coconut Meatballs; brown rice; Cabbage with Coconut Vinegar

Standard U.S./Metric Measurement Conversions

VOLUME CONVERSIONS	
U.S. Volume Measure	**Metric Equivalent**
⅛ teaspoon	0.5 milliliters
¼ teaspoon	1 milliliters
½ teaspoon	2 milliliters
1 teaspoon	5 milliliters
½ tablespoon	7 milliliters
1 tablespoon (3 teaspoons)	15 milliliters
2 tablespoons (1 fluid ounce)	30 milliliters
¼ cup (4 tablespoons)	60 milliliters
⅓ cup	90 milliliters
½ cup (4 fluid ounces)	125 milliliters
⅔ cup	160 milliliters
¾ cup (6 fluid ounces)	180 milliliters
1 cup (16 tablespoons)	250 milliliters
1 pint (2 cups)	500 milliliters
1 quart (4 cups)	1 liter (about)

WEIGHT CONVERSIONS	
U.S. Weight Measure	**Metric Equivalent**
½ ounce	15 grams
1 ounce	30 grams
2 ounces	60 grams
3 ounces	85 grams
¼ pound (4 ounces)	115 grams
½ pound (8 ounces)	225 grams
¾ pound (12 ounces)	340 grams
1 pound (16 ounces)	454 grams

Standard U.S./Metric Measurement Conversions

OVEN TEMPERATURE CONVERSIONS	
Degrees Fahrenheit	**Degrees Celsius**
200 degrees F	95 degrees C
250 degrees F	120 degrees C
275 degrees F	135 degrees C
300 degrees F	150 degrees C
325 degrees F	160 degrees C
350 degrees F	180 degrees C
375 degrees F	190 degrees C
400 degrees F	205 degrees C
425 degrees F	220 degrees C
450 degrees F	230 degrees C

BAKING PAN SIZES	
American	**Metric**
8 x 1½ inch round baking pan	20 x 4 cm cake tin
9 x 1½ inch round baking pan	23 x 3.5 cm cake tin
1 x 7 x 1½ inch baking pan	28 x 18 x 4 cm baking tin
13 x 9 x 2 inch baking pan	30 x 20 x 5 cm baking tin
2 quart rectangular baking dish	30 x 20 x 3 cm baking tin
15 x 10 x 2 inch baking pan	30 x 25 x 2 cm baking tin (Swiss roll tin)
9 inch pie plate	22 x 4 or 23 x 4 cm pie plate
7 or 8 inch springform pan	18 or 20 cm springform or loose bottom cake tin
9 x 5 x 3 inch loaf pan	23 x 13 x 7 cm or 2 lb narrow loaf or pate tin
1½ quart casserole	1.5 litre casserole
2 quart casserole	2 litre casserole

General Index

Index of Recipes

Note: Since all recipes contain coconut, only those with coconut as a primary ingredient are listed under the main entry Coconut. Otherwise, the recipes are listed under their main ingredient(s) or category of food (Side dishes, Salads, etc.). Page numbers in **bold** indicate recipe category lists.

We Have

EVERYTHING

on Anything!

With more than 19 million copies sold, the Everything® series has become one of America's favorite resources for solving problems, learning new skills, and organizing lives. Our brand is not only recognizable—it's also welcomed.

The series is a hand-in-hand partner for people who are ready to tackle new subjects—like you!

For more information on the Everything® series, please visit *www.adamsmedia.com*

The Everything® list spans a wide range of subjects, with more than 500 titles covering 25 different categories:

Business	History	Reference
Careers	Home Improvement	Religion
Children's Storybooks	Everything Kids	Self-Help
Computers	Languages	Sports & Fitness
Cooking	Music	Travel
Crafts and Hobbies	New Age	Wedding
Education/Schools	Parenting	Writing
Games and Puzzles	Personal Finance	
Health	Pets	